How
Beowulf
Can Save
America

HOW BEOWULF CAN SAVE AMERICA

An Epic Hero's Guide to Defeating the Politics of Rage

BY ROBIN R. BATES

New York: Discovering Oz Press
2012

ISBN-13: 978-1478113775
ISBN-10: 1478113774

To Rachel Kranz,
Dear friend and the best coach I've ever known

—·—·—·—·—·—·—

"Effective political stories have four fundamental elements: a villain, a threat, a hero, and a vision. When these four parts are clear and compelling, a story has the power to move people to take action."

— Van Jones, *Rebuild the Dream*

—·—·—·—·—·—·—

Contents

PREFACE

I'm not sure when I first consciously realized that stories are not just stories but also survival tools. Perhaps it was when I was nine and Frodo showed me that I could be valiant, even though I was small and the target of bullies. Perhaps it was when, at 11, Huck Finn and Scout Finch let me know that I didn't have to experience Tennessee's bitter desegregation battles alone because they too were upset by racism. Perhaps it was when I was 15 and saw that Holden Caulfield understood my fear that no one, no catcher in the rye, would save me from running off the cliff of childhood.

It was in college, however, that I learned how to talk about the impact of stories. *Beowulf* got me started. Phil Niles, Carleton College's medieval history professor, told us that *Beowulf's* monsters were more than literary characters for ninth-century Anglo-Saxon warriors. Monsters were their way to articulate the unsolvable problems that were tearing their society apart. Grendel and Grendel's Mother, he said, represented the unending blood feuds that kept kingdoms in a perpetual state of unrest, while the dragon that shows up towards the end of the poem embodied the greed within kings that undermined social stability.

Suddenly I had evidence for something I had

always instinctively known: literature is a guide for dealing with our most pressing problems. *Beowulf* and other literary works were not merely flights of fancy or beautiful verbal constructions. They were road maps that could help us navigate difficult terrain, both in the world around us and deep within our own souls. Literature, I saw, was not just enjoyable entertainment but a crucial means of engaging with life.

Since that long-ago college history class, I never lost my fondness for *Beowulf,* and over the years I have learned that its impact is not limited to medieval warriors. As a college English professor who has been teaching the poem for over 25 years, I have witnessed scores of students applying it to their lives in countless ways. I was therefore not surprised when a new translation of *Beowulf* climbed onto the *New York Times* bestseller list in 2000 and when two *Beowulf* films were made in the decade that followed. I can even report that, in my own darkest hour, the poem came to my aid. After I lost my eldest son in a drowning accident, I came to appreciate how deeply *Beowulf* speaks to sorrow. Just as the poem's hero wrestles with a figure of grief at the bottom of a dark lake, so I descended into my own dark place and confronted emotions that threatened to hold me under and destroy me. As I reread the poem in the tumultuous weeks following Justin's death, I took heart from Beowulf's victory and vowed that, like him, I would do everything in my power to return to the light.

Three years ago I launched a blog dedicated to showing how classic literature can change our lives. In honor of the work that had meant so much to me, I named the blog *Better Living through Beowulf.* Six days a week I find a literary work that illumines a contemporary issue or news item and post a short essay applying literature to life. *Beowulf,* it so happens, has shown up in my blog more than any other work, although the masterpieces of Shakespeare, Austen, Dickens, Dostoevsky, Homer, Twain, Fielding, Donne, Herbert and others are also well represented, as are contemporary authors and poets, humorists, and, on "Film Friday," a wide variety of classic, popular, and foreign films.

My blog came into being not long after Barack Obama took office, and last year, when reading back over my posts, I noticed that I had particularly relied upon *Beowulf* to make sense of the political turmoil surrounding the Obama presidency. I was appalled by the irrational attacks on a president whose efforts to generate hope and inspire change I greatly admired, and I was puzzled by the depth and intensity of grief and rage that his presidency seemed to evoke. *Beowulf,* as it happened, helped me view these responses with more clarity as I struggled to come to terms with them. Through my blog I wanted to create a different type of discussion than could be found in most op-ed pieces or political journals.

Although I write daily on literature's applicability to modern life, even I was surprised by the extent to which *Beowulf* helped me chart the resentment, rage, and grief that drive so much of the irrational opposition to the president (as opposed to the more reasoned criticisms of him and his policies). In retrospect, however, it makes sense that *Beowulf* would have something important to say. When people have lost their bearings, monster stories are particularly powerful at capturing the chaos within.

I wanted to explore these ideas further and in more depth than I could achieve in my blog. At the suggestion of my son and publisher Darien Bates, I embarked on a book that would explore whether *Beowulf* has answers for contemporary America. Having spent most of the past year working on this project, I can confidently say that it does.

At first I thought the book would be about overcoming our anger and rediscovering a 1950s sense of civility. As I burrowed into the monsters' relevance to our situation, however, I realized that our incivility is a symptom of the current state of affairs, not the cause. Aided by my friend Rachel Kranz, I concluded that America today has a dragon problem not unrelated to medieval England's greedy king dilemma. If Americans find themselves possessed by *Beowulf's* monsters of resentment, sorrow, and despair, it is because we have contemporary dragons that are hoarding America's wealth.

Each election, it seems, becomes more critical than the one before. That's because the growing income gap between the wealthy and the rest of the country is causing America to become increasingly dysfunctional. As citizens of a democracy, we all have the responsibility to learn what we can about the monsters besieging our country and to battle them. At the very least, we must vote. This book offers you *Beowulf*'s tips for fighting our contemporary versions of the poem's trolls and dragons. The time has come for concerned citizens to take up arms, restore the integrity of our political process, and reclaim our democracy.

I wish to acknowledge the many, many people who have helped me with this book, beginning with the students in my various British Literature survey courses, my English colleagues, and my faculty writing group.

While I am no political scientist, I work to be an informed citizen and for that rely on *The New York Times*, *The Washington Post*, *The New Yorker*, *The New York Review of Books*, and other publications to keep track of political developments. I am grateful to a number of political writers who help me sort through the issues I explore in this book, including Andrew Sullivan and David Frum of *The Daily Beast*; E. J. Dionne, Gene Robinson, Ezra Klein, and Harold Meyerson of *The Washington Post*; Paul Krugman, Gail Collins, David Brooks, and Maureen Dowd of *The New York Times*; Jonathan Cohn and Timothy Noah of *The New Republic*; Jonathan Chait of *New York Magazine*; Ryan Lizza, John Cassidy, and Nicholas Lemann of *The New Yorker*; Steve Benen of *The Maddow Blog*; Robert Reich and Thomas Frank; and a host of others.

For the *Beowulf* material, I wish to thank the various *Beowulf* scholars whose work I have absorbed over the years; William Bolton for making sure that what I say about the poem is in accord with recent scholarship (any mistakes are my own, however); and W. W. Norton for allowing me to use passages from Seamus Heaney's remarkable translation.

For the book itself, I thank Chris Kalb for his cover art and book-design skills; my son Darien for giving me the idea and then supporting and guiding me through the process; my son Toby for being an invaluable cheerleader and a sounding board for ideas (Toby and Darien have been my Wiglafs); Jackie Paskow for reading over drafts; Steve Ryan for a fascinating discussion on the U.S. economy; Rachel Kranz for alternatively encouraging me and pushing me to the next level; and above all my wife Julia for reading drafts, suggesting that I write this foreword, and putting up with an abstracted husband. Often they have seemed to me like the warriors who accept Beowulf's invitation to crowd into a small vessel and sail off to a foreign land to battle angry trolls. When I have lost faith and suggested that we turn back, they have urged me on. They all have my deep gratitude.

INTRODUCTION

In the eyes of many bewildered observers, the current Republican Party has been taken over by a mysterious alien force. As I write this in April of 2012, we can look back at a primary season where Republican candidates for president vied for who could stake out the most extreme position on a range of issues and who accused the president of everything from infanticide to, in effect, treason. Meanwhile, Republican legislators who are long-time moderates or reasonable conservatives have moved rapidly to the right to forestall challenges from their party's right wing, making compromise between the two parties all but impossible. America may be trying to dig itself out of its greatest economic crisis since the Great Depression, but certain Republican members of Congress have been doing all in their power to gum up the works, including threatening credit default, filibustering routine bills, delaying or rejecting even uncontroversial appointments, voting against measures they used to support, and disavowing Keynesian stimulus solutions they once believed in.

In *It's Even Worse Than It Looks*, Washington political analysts Thomas Mann of the bipartisan Brookings Institution and Norman Ornstein of the conservative American Enterprise Institute are devastatingly succinct:

> One of our two major parties, the Republicans, has
> become an insurgent outlier—ideologically extreme,
> contemptuous of the inherited social and economic
> policy regime, scornful of compromise, unpersuaded
> by conventional understanding of facts, evidence and
> science, and dismissive of the legitimacy of its polit-
> ical opposition (qtd. in Lizza 38).

Destructive though the strategy has been to national cohesion,
it has delivered political rewards. Through their maneuvering,
Republicans managed to slow Democratic momentum in 2009
and to post large gains in the 2010 off-year elections. They've
paid a price—at times Congress's approval ratings have dropped
to single digits—but they've managed to drag the president down
with them. Barack Obama's glowing vision of hope and change
hangs like a tattered banner over a bloody battlefield, his various
accomplishments all but drowned out by the shouting. "Yes, we
can" appears to have been replaced by "No, we can't."

Enter *Beowulf* to the rescue. This 1000-year-old Anglo-Saxon
warrior poem, one of the world's great epics, specializes in monstrous rage, capturing that destructive emotion in all its madness
and intensity. The poem features three monsters, each with its
modern-day equivalent of a political problem that is contributing
to our current morass. Fortunately, *Beowulf* also has a hero who
knows what to do if there's a monster in the house. When it comes
to understanding our contentiousness and providing steps for
overcoming it, *Beowulf* does a better job than the advice of colum-
nists and political science prescriptions. As such, it can function
as a guide for all Democrats, Republicans, and Independents who
wish to get the country working again.

You don't need to be familiar with *Beowulf* to benefit from this
book. In the following pages I walk you through the poem and
highlight the applicable scenes and passages. I have also provided
two appendices: a plot summary and a list of the characters alluded
to, many of whose names confusingly begin with the letter "H."

To defeat the politics of rage, we must go to the root of the problem. In the first two monsters that Beowulf battles, a troll and his mother, we can see the resentment and the angry grieving that are tearing our country apart. But it is the third monster, the dragon, that reveals our underlying malaise. In Anglo-Saxon times, society had a dragon problem when it experienced discrepancies in wealth that its people perceived as grossly unfair. Greedy kings were regarded as dragons whose hoarding undermined the society's sense of unity. In America today, middle-class income stagnation and a growing gap between the middle class and the very wealthy have led to dissension such as we have not seen since the early days of the Great Depression.

Addressing the causes of this monstrous anger will not only restore a semblance of political peace to our beleaguered nation. It will also allow us to look once again toward the future. In the poem, Beowulf's victory over the dragon liberates a cave filled with immense riches. If wealth were once again to flow freely through America, we could rebuild a country that answers to our needs and dreams.

How do we size up our monsters and figure out a battle plan? *Beowulf* leads the way.

THE COUNTRY UNDER SIEGE

As we look back to the early days of Barack Obama's presidency, we might well conclude that the president brought the wrong weapons to the fight. In 2008 he believed, along with many Americans, that simple outreach could lead the country past its bitter partisan divides and into a new era of cooperation. "There is not a liberal America and a conservative America—," he declared in his acceptance speech at the Democratic National Convention, "there is the United States of America." In Obama's vision, people would reach beyond their antagonisms to find a common purpose. It would take work, of course—as a former community organizer and U.S. senator, Obama knew that people are often driven by self-interest—but he thought that most of us would realize that collaboration benefited everyone. His job, as he saw it, was to get everyone to the table where they could engage in bipartisan negotiating.

We now know that events didn't unfold as the president had hoped. Instead of witnessing a new spirit, America saw its political divides grow yet more toxic. Angry trolls rampaged through America's mead hall, and the brave young warrior who was supposed to clean up the mess became a discouraged king presiding over it.

Obama should have read *Beowulf*.

If he had, he would have seen the anger directed against him in all of its destructive intransigence. Literature, Shakespeare memorably writes, holds a mirror up to nature, and *Beowulf* is particularly adept at mirroring rage. The epic's genius lies in the way it grasps the essence of destructive anger, distilling it into unforgettable figures. Mere human characters wouldn't capture the insanity half as well as *Beowulf*'s nightmarish creatures.

The poem also understands how anger strips us of our humanity and turns us into monsters. Through vivid depictions of Grendel, Grendel's Mother, and the dragon, Americans can see what we are up against. We learn, for instance, that anger takes at least three different forms, each with its own characteristic mode of attack and each posing a distinctive threat to society. We also learn that each manifestation of anger must be fought in a particular way.

The poem understands anger because it was written during a time that was intimately acquainted with violence. Anglo-Saxon society regularly witnessed skirmishes between neighboring kingdoms, not to mention battles against invading Vikings. If hostile warriors overran a village, all its citizens could be killed or enslaved. The society experienced internal instances of violence as well, often in the form of interminable blood feuds. Fighting could also break out after the death of a king, with different relatives and warriors vying to succeed him.

In America today we do not face threats of death and enslavement. We do, however, face a roiling anger that is undermining our governing institutions, setting citizen against citizen, and preventing collective problem-solving. In its account of Beowulf battling and defeating the three monsters, the epic captures our own situation and shows us how to deal with it.

AMERICA'S MONSTERS

The first monster, Grendel, represents angry resentment. Grendel is a giant troll who is driven mad by the merriment of others. Excluded as he is from the great mead hall where King Hrothgar distributes the society's wealth, he writhes in envy. Significantly, he doesn't touch the king's throne when he invades the hall, which is to say he doesn't vent his anger against the wealth-distributing system. He directs it rather towards the beneficiaries of the king's largesse, the king's warriors, whom he butchers and devours in a blind rage.

We see a comparable rage in those American citizens who verbally lash out at neighbors who they think have been unfairly granted privileges. Over the past three years, such resentful rage has been directed against, among others, undocumented workers, American Muslims, African Americans, Latinos and Latinas, teachers, government workers, union members, delinquent home-owners, Planned Parenthood clients, and food stamp recipients. Every day, it seems, new groups are added to the list. When it comes to certain scapegoats in America today, otherwise decent people harden over and say ugly things. Grendelian resentment thus has the power to rend the social fabric.

Beowulf's second monster alerts us to the fact that angry resentment doesn't travel alone. It is accompanied—indeed, it has been birthed—by grief. Although Beowulf manages to kill Grendel, retaliation arrives the very next night in the form of Grendel's vengeful mother. The connection between the two monsters leads us to realize that resentment always contains an element of sorrow. Grendel and Grendel's mother function as an inextricable pair.

Many Americans possessed by Grendel's resentment also feel that they have lost something close to their hearts. Look closely at the anger directed against fellow citizens and you will usually find at its core a grieving for a lost America. Many extol the virtues of a previous golden age, which in their view can look like idealized versions of 1950s suburbia, the small-government frontier West, the America of the Founding Fathers, and occasionally even the antebellum South. Grendel's Mother may strike second in the poem, but she precedes resentful rage and lives deep within us.

The poem's final monster is the dragon, which makes its appearance late in Beowulf's reign as a successful king. The dragon is the emblem of a culture in which wealth no longer circulates freely and where people have ceased to be generous. Dragons are scaly hard, venomous, angry, and self-absorbed. Dragonhood is particularly debilitating because it represents the triumph of cynicism over idealism. When a society loses hope in its future, people retreat into their lairs, determined to at least protect what they already have.

Beowulf's portrayal of the dragon invites us to identify and explore despair, which might be our deepest anger. The poem is also a call to explore the greed and the unequal distribution of wealth out of which cynicism and desperation arise. In Anglo-Saxon society, society's basic social contract called for warriors to be loyal to their kings and for kings to generously redistribute the wealth that warriors brought in. If a king began to hoard instead of share, warrior loyalty was strained, uncertainty entered the picture, and gloom descended.

America has its own version of this basic contract and its own version of dragon greed. According to former Clinton Secretary of Labor Robert Reich in *Aftershock*, all goes well when the nation provides its workers with enough money to buy what they produce (42-43). Such was the situation during what Reich calls "the Great Prosperity of 1947-1975." In the 1980's, however, the

American middle class was hit by "the double whammy of global competition and labor-replacing technologies" (6), leading the country to take what could be described as dragon austerity measures. We did not, Reich notes, strengthen safety nets, empower labor unions, improve education and job training, and figure out other ways to adapt the American work force. Instead, we "embraced deregulation and privatization, attacked and diminished labor unions, cut taxes on the wealthy, and shredded social safety nets" (54-55).

As a result, Reich argues, we saw stagnant wages for most Americans, increasing job insecurity, and steadily widening inequality. By 2007, the top one percent of the country took in a staggering 23.5 percent of the nation's total income—a drastic increase from their less than nine percent share in the late 1970s (*Aftershock,* 6). Today, the top 400 people in America have as much money as the bottom 150 million ("Widening Gap").

A major result of the recent recession has been to push an even higher percentage of the nation's wealth into the upper income brackets. In 2010, the first year of the recovery, Berkeley economist Emmanuel Saez reports that the top one percent of Americans captured 93 percent of the income gains (4). This occurred at a time when states were (as they still are) laying off teachers and government employees, hiking the cost of college tuitions, rescinding pension agreements, cutting back on Medicaid reimbursements, closing state parks, and engaging in other stringent cost-cutting measures. In short, the richest Americans have more money than they can spend while the rest of the country is experiencing deepening discontent and, in Reich's words, "ever nastier politics" (*Aftershock* 76).

These, then, are the dimensions of America's rage: resentment, grief, and despair. The monsters that attack Beowulf and his world illuminate the monsters we face today.

Nor does the poem only help us identify our angers. Through a plethora of plots and subplots involving various kings, queens, and warriors, it also teaches us *how* one becomes a monster. The poem includes a bewildering array of minor characters, but they are important for our purposes because they show us, step by step, the process of transformation from a calm and rational neighbor to a bitter and enraged antagonist.

Beowulf helps us see that if Americans are directing their fire against each other, it is because we feel torn apart and devoured by resentment, dragged into a deep mire by a sense of loss, and locked in a dark cave by cynicism. In other words, Grendel, Grendel's Mother, and the dragon are doing a number on us.

A HERO WHO CAN SAVE US

Beowulf doesn't stop with the monsters, however. It affirms that the anger can be defeated and that America doesn't have to be like this. It shows us who we must be to triumph.

In the following pages, I devote each of the odd-numbered chapters to a different monster—resentful Grendel, grief-stricken Grendel's Mother, the cynical dragon—and explore how they are possessing American citizens and wreaking havoc on the nation. In the even-numbered chapters, I look at how Beowulf counters the monsters, examining which strategies get the job done and which don't.

Beowulf shows us that there are always two battles to be fought. First, we must find ways to win over or neutralize those of our monster-infested compatriots who are damaging our institutions and, upon occasion, directing their rage at us. Yet if we are to be effective heroes, we must also overcome the monsters that lurk within ourselves. We all have monster potential—the monster is always the hero's dark double—and we are frequently tempted to harden over and resort to the same tactics employed by those who rage against us. If so, we will not end the madness but perpetuate it.

Applying *Beowulf's* insights to this second challenge, progressives and moderates can learn that remaining calm and holding fast to principles of integrity work better against resentment than angry rejoinders. After all, in the face of stout resolve, resentment can lose confidence and disintegrate. Progressives and moderates will further learn that destructive grief loses its steam when we begin to act upon the truths that the signers of *The Declaration of Independence* found to be self-evident, truths that point the way back to a more egalitarian and less divided country. They will learn finally that, although we can't fight a greedy dragon alone, if we join with others, especially with young people, we can purge ourselves of cynicism's venom and go on to build a fair and open society.

We hear our call to arms midway through the poem. Danish King Hrothgar is in a wretched state, his hopes having been dashed by a second monster attack. After momentarily believing, as many believed on Obama's election night, that monstrous resentment is dead and he can finally sleep easy, Hrothgar loses his best friend to monstrous grieving. "Rest, what is rest?" he cries out piteously as he mourns the death of Aeschere. "Sorrow has returned."

The young Beowulf is at first unsettled by the sight of an old and revered king in despair. Then, displaying a maturity beyond his years, he all but tells Hrothgar to get a grip. "Bear up," he commands, "and be the man I expect you to be."

We should all expect ourselves to be men and women who rise to the occasion. Yes, there is much to be discouraged about, but self-pity is a luxury we cannot afford. Fortunately, *Beowulf* provides us with the guidance and the inspiration we need to shake off our doldrums and march to the aid of our country. Think of the poem as a handbook for modern-day citizen warriors.

Chapter 1

GRENDEL: JEALOUS RESENTMENT

Resentment against minorities, the poor, and other vulnerable groups has been at work in America from the beginning, but it has seldom been used to sabotage the act of governing. Since 2009, however, certain members of the Republican Party have used the angry resentment of the Tea Party movement to stymie the Democrats while discouraging their own flock from making the compromises upon which successful governance depends.

Many trace the Tea Party's rise to a resentful rant on the floor of the Chicago mercantile exchange by CNBC commentator Rick Santelli. Declaring that President Barack Obama's mortgage bailout plan was promoting "bad behavior" and turning the United States into Cuba, Santelli cried out to Chicago traders, "This is America! How many of you people want to pay for your neighbors' mortgage that has an extra bathroom and can't pay their bills? ... President Obama, are you listening?!"

Suddenly the prevailing narrative had it that the government was unfairly helping irresponsible citizens while ignoring "hardworking Americans," and those losing homes found themselves attacked as people looking for a free ride. Although many houses were foreclosed because the owners had lost their jobs and even more because bankers made empty assurances while issuing imprudent or even fraudulent loans, the real culprits were declared to be deadbeat borrowers, with the government cast as an irresponsible enabler. A significant number of Americans were moved to righteous fury, and opposition to Obama discovered its voice.

The targets of the fury are not only foreclosed homeowners. Every week, it seems, Tea Party Republicans, guided by right-wing commentators and unscrupulous candidates, single out a different group as posing a supposed threat to America. One week we hear complaints about fraudulent voters; the next, we hear attacks upon undeserving recipients of food stamps; then the villains are low-income earners who don't pay income taxes. Next we are told that American Muslims want to impose Sharia law on fellow citizens, that same-sex couples are undermining the sanctity of marriage, and that public sector retirees are bankrupting municipalities.

These words have sometimes been backed up by state laws and ballot initiatives. We have seen the passage of draconian anti-immigrant legislation in Arizona and Alabama; the suspension of collective bargaining rights in Wisconsin and Indiana; the recall of judges who ruled in favor of same-sex marriage in Iowa; and the denial to Muslims of the right to build mosques in New York and Tennessee. Fearing that people "unlike us" are taking over the country, thirteen states have instituted picture identification laws designed to suppress voter turnout.

In their recent book *Crashing the Tea Party*, Paul Street and Anthony DiMaggio identify the major constituents of the Tea Party as middle- and upper middle-class whites. They are filled with rage at being excluded from the tremendous economic prosperity they see the richest Americans having achieved and at the same time fear that those below them will take away the wealth that they do have. Ironically, a number of the angriest citizens are themselves beneficiaries of state-sponsored Medicare and Social Security who fear that government support for others will cut their own benefits. They are thus susceptible to what Street and DiMaggio describe as a "top-down manufactured rage, created and disseminated by a combination of official, corporate, and media-based voices at the expense of genuine grassroots empowerment" (44). The irony, as the authors point out, is that the "probusiness policies" advocated by these voices will only exacerbate anxieties by "accelerat[ing] the dramatic growth of inequality and stagnation of working- and middle-class incomes that have occurred over the last four decades" (44-45).

A DEMON NURSING A HARD GRIEVANCE

Grendel provides a handle for understanding Tea Partiers and other angry Americans. Think of the monster not as an actual individual but as an archetype of resentful rage. He is the monstrous urge within anxious and vulnerable people to strike out at those they think are receiving special favors. Feeling perpetually neglected, Grendel dwells on imagined slights:

> Then a powerful demon, a prowler through the dark,
> nursed a hard grievance. It harrowed him
> to hear the din of the loud banquet
> every day in the hall, the harp being struck
> and the clear song of a skilled poet . . .

Aggrieved individuals experience a powerful adrenaline rush when they vent their wrath against others. To apply to them the poem's description of a Grendel attack, they sense that flames are shooting from their eyes and may fantasize about obliterating their enemies in a blind fury:

—.—.—.—.—.—.—.—

Spurned and joyless, [Grendel] journeyed on ahead
and arrived at the hawn. The iron-braced door
turned on its hinge when his hands touched it.
Then his rage boiled over, he ripped open
the mouth of the building, maddening for blood,
pacing the length of the patterned floor
with his loathsome tread, while a baleful light,
flame more than light, flared from his eyes.
He saw many men in the mansion, sleeping,
a ranked company of kinsmen and warriors
quartered together. And his glee was demonic,
picturing the mayhem: before morning
he would rip life from limb and devour them,
feed on their flesh...

—.—.—.—.—.—.—.—

A ninth-century warrior possessed with Grendelian resentment
might well grab a sword and vent his murderous rage upon fellow
warriors. I imagine such a man, perhaps befuddled with drink and
suffering from PTSD, succumbing to his inner Grendel during an
argument about who is more deserving of the king's bounty. Our
own Grendel-crazed compatriots don't generally murder people,
but their political misbehavior is undermining civil discourse and
preventing leaders from governing responsibly. Far too many
politicians, pundits, bloggers and "ordinary citizens" feel they
have license to say repellent things about America's scapegoats,
regardless of the consequences.

Not only national politics are affected. The ripple effects are
hitting state houses, legislatures, county commissions, court-
houses, school boards, even church vestries. Grendel takes over
individuals, who proceed to shout ideological slogans rather than
collaborate with, let alone become friends with, those of other
races, ethnicities, nationalities, classes, and sexual preferences.

Through several minor characters, *Beowulf* shows us what it looks like when humans are infected with Grendelian resentment. The Danish warrior Unferth is exhibit #1.

HOTHEADED RANTING

When Beowulf walks into King Hrothgar's hall and promises to slay Grendel, a high-ranking official who sits at Hrothgar's feet takes umbrage. Unferth is less concerned with the nation's problems than with being displaced by a young upstart:

—·—·—·—·—·—·—·—·—

Beowulf's coming,
his sea-braving, made him sick with envy:
he could not brook or abide the fact
that anyone else alive under heaven
might enjoy greater regard than he did...

—·—·—·—·—·—·—·—·—

At a moment when the Danes are experiencing hope for the first time in years and are willing to give Beowulf a chance, Unferth proceeds to do everything he can to tear the young hero down. Think of Unferth's attack as a symptom of a deeper rage loose in the land. Beowulf is a fraud, Unferth claims, and he tells a story about how Beowulf foolhardily engaged in a swimming match with a friend. Not only was Beowulf foolish, Unferth adds, but he lost the race.

Unferth fits the profile of what business writer Robert Sutton has memorably described as "the asshole in the office." In *The No Asshole Rule: Building a Civilized Workplace and Surviving One That Isn't*, Sutton describes the damage that such individuals can accomplish. Unferth is a warrior who has killed some of his own relatives, and in a modern setting perhaps he would "stab a colleague in the back." With Beowulf, he uses classic bullying tactics to wield disproportionate influence. The American political scene is currently crawling with Unferths.

In the next chapter I will examine the means by which Beowulf faces down Unferth and turns him into an ally. The episode provides us with an important guide for working with our own resentful fellow citizens. Before doing so, however, let me introduce another character who proves more intractable than Unferth and who, when we encounter him in our own lives, requires more careful handling. Hrothulf, King Hrothgar's nephew, is a murderous schemer.

COLD-BLOODED SCHEMING

If King Hrothgar dies before his boys are of age, Hrothulf will become the regent. He is jealous of them, and they are still young when Hrothgar indeed dies early. As regent, Hrothulf stages a coup, kills one of the sons, and attempts to kill the other. Eventually he himself is killed, but during the civil strife the great Hall of Heorot, symbol of national unity and Danish prowess, burns to the ground.

If Unferth is the guy who mouths hate speech in a bar, Hrothulf is the plotter who does real systemic damage. We will see that each of the three monsters in *Beowulf* has a hot and a cold form—when they are not raging through the land, they are brooding sullenly in their lairs. So think of Unferth as the hot form of resentment while Regent Hrothulf is the cold. A modern-day political equivalent of Unferth might be Alan West, a Florida Congressman and Tea Party favorite who once told liberals to "get the hell out of America." Hrothulf, on the other hand, could be the far more effective Senate Minority Leader Mitch McConnell, who has said his major goal "is for President Obama to be a one-term president" and who has figured that bogging down all Congressional legislation will result in disenchantment with Obama, leading to a Republican president. In Unferth and Hrothulf we see clearly the two types of challenge that resentment poses for America: one man speaks his resentment, the other man cold-bloodedly plots to act it out.

The next chapter shows how, by tapping into Beowulf's mind-set and Beowulf's tactics, we can defeat the Grendel-possessed Unferths and Hrothulfs that are fracturing political discourse. Before we move into battle, however, let us first acknowledge how powerless we can feel when such figures are on a rampage.

AMERICA IN DESPAIR

More than a few Americans will find an image of themselves in the description of King Hrothgar, who is despondent over resentment's toll:

—·—·—·—·—·—·—·—

Their mighty prince,
the storied leader, sat stricken and helpless,
humiliated by the loss of his guard,
bewildered and stunned, staring aghast
at the demon's trail, in deep distress.
He was numb with grief, but got no respite
for one night later merciless Grendel
struck again with more gruesome murders.

—·—·—·—·—·—·—·—

Do you recognize here any of your own despair? And now, to remind yourself how urgent it is to achieve clarity and to devise an effective plan of action, think of how frustrated you've felt when you've heard politicians and commentators repeatedly proffer the same meaningless "solutions." Today we hear ritual invocations of "family values," "tax cuts," and "keeping the country safe," just as in the poem King Hrothgar's counselors worship at pagan shrines and swear oaths to the devil. The advice Hrothgar gets, like such advice today, appears to have little chance of working:

———·——·——·——·——·——·——

          powerful counselors,
the highest in the land, would lend advice,
plotting how best the bold defenders
might resist and beat off sudden attacks.
Sometimes at pagan shrines they vowed
offerings to idols, swore oaths
that the killer of souls [the devil] might come to their aid
and save the people.

———·——·——·——·——·——·——

So that's where we stand. Grendel fury has entered certain
Americans, who are venting their rage on their fellow citizens.
The great mead hall that is America may not burn to the ground,
as does Heorot Hall during Regent Hrothulf's fratricidal coup,
but it is taking a beating. How we are to respond as warriors is
the subject of the next chapter.

Chapter 2

BEOWULF'S RESPONSE: A FIRM GRIP

Upon first glance, a young tough-talking warrior who purges King Hrothgar's mead hall of its monsters might seem a fantasy solution to divisiveness, not a real one. Both Democrats and Republicans periodically indulge in this fantasy, however. Many of us respond deeply to the story of the fresh outsider who rides into town and brings a fractious community together. When the problems seem so intractable that our king and his counselors are at a loss, we may long for a savior untainted by Washington.

The reason Beowulf succeeds, however—the reason he is a true epic hero and not just a fresh new face—is that he possesses a set of crucial qualities that enable him to defeat each incarnation of monstrous rage that he encounters. Indeed, Beowulf represents precisely those qualities that all Americans must cultivate if we are to prevail against the resentment that plagues us. If our leaders and if we as citizens are to stand tall against racism, homophobia, anti-immigrant hysteria, attacks against food stamp recipients, anti-Muslim fear-mongering, and other forms taken by American resentment, we must begin acting like Beowulf. We must learn to hold our ground, engage intimately with the rage so that we under stand it, and assert with a firm grip our vision of *e pluribus unum*. If we do, we can begin building a nation where all treat each other with respect. Out of many, we can convince our fellow citizens, we are one.

What should you do if you encounter a colleague spouting hate-filled resentment or see an elected representative advocating resentment-driven legislation? The archetypal battle between Beowulf and Grendel provides a blueprint on how to respond.

STEPS FOR BATTLING RESENTMENT

Before engaging, Beowulf makes some deliberate decisions:

⫸ he first examines how the monster operates. When Grendel comes storming into the hall where Beowulf and his men are sleeping, Beowulf stays still and watches the monster at work. After Grendel seizes and devours one of his men, Beowulf understands that the monster is pitiless and cannot be reasoned with;

⫸ he does not opt for the solution that his men take, which is to hack at Grendel with their swords. Their unfocused attacks mirror the attacks of Grendelian resentment itself, a response that the poem finds to be useless:

> [N]o blade on earth, no blacksmith's art
> could ever damage their demon opponent.
> He had conjured the harm from the cutting edge
> of every weapon.

⫸ instead, Beowulf stays grounded and "seizes" his opportunity when it presents itself, grabbing Grendel's hand and refusing to let go;

⫸ Beowulf's grip is both firm and intimate. He comes to know the monster *mano a mano*;

⠀⠀⠀⟫→ when the monster realizes that Beowulf is strong in his resolve, he loses his former bravado and panics. To escape, Grendel tears himself free of his arm, sustaining a mortal wound and ensuring Beowulf's victory. The hoped-for outcome, in other words (I massage the metaphor a little at this point), is that the resentment rips itself free from the individual and retreats to a dark cave, or to a place deep inside. The warrior is thereby freed to shake hands with Beowulf.

⠀⠀⠀Of course, we should not literally arm-wrestle with our fellow Americans when we see them spewing invective. But the battle between Grendel and Beowulf captures, in a scene that few readers ever forget, the intensity of struggling with Grendelian resentment and the necessity of remaining steadfast.

⠀⠀⠀Standing up to a resentment-crazed antagonist is not easy. An iconic image that comes to mind is African-American student Elizabeth Eckford walking with dignity to newly integrated Little Rock Central High School in 1957 as onlookers heckle her. One of these hecklers, her face contorted with anger, is white classmate Hazel Bryan. Years later Eckford and Bryan would shake hands.

⠀⠀⠀If Grendel is the archetype of resentment and Beowulf the archetype of steadfast courage, then in Beowulf's confrontation with Unferth we see what happens when the archetypes fight it out in a situation we can relate to. We can adapt Beowulf's Grendel-fighting skills to "disarm" our fellow Unferths.

CONFRONTING A BULLY

Unferth, as we have seen, seethes with Grendelian envy and resentment, taunting Beowulf the moment he walks into King Hrothgar's hall. Here's how Beowulf handles him:

⠀⠀⠀⟫→ Beowulf does not respond impulsively. Rather, he steps back, assesses the situation, and notices that Unferth has been drinking:

—.—.—.—.—.—.—.—.

> Well, friend Unferth, you have had your say
> about Breca and me. But it was mostly beer
> that was doing the talking.

—.—.—.—.—.—.—.—.

⁂→ Beowulf then seizes the initiative, correcting the record by telling what really happened;

⁂→ he affirms his own strengths in a clear and straightforward manner (his strong grip);

⁂→ he exposes Unferth's vulnerabilities, noting his spotted past ("you killed your own kith and kin") and pointing out that Unferth's approach can't solve the current problems;

⁂→ after Beowulf kills Grendel, he proves a gracious winner and does not rub his victory in Unferth's face;

⁂→ as a result, Unferth makes peace with his former enemy. When Beowulf sets off to fight Grendel's Mother, Unferth presents him with a valuable sword.

We can learn several things from this encounter. First, upon being baited by Unferth, Beowulf remains centered and calm and (as in the battle with Grendel) does not reach for his sword. He understands that, when we react to anger with anger, Anger wins. This is why Grendel can "conjure the harm" from the warriors' swords. Unferth would gain the upper hand if he managed to provoke Beowulf since his envy and resentment would poison the encounter.

Second, Beowulf uses eloquence to defeat Unferth, showing us that leadership calls for rhetorical skills. Beowulf may refrain from anger but he goes on the verbal attack:

—.—.—.—.—.—.—.—.

> The fact is, Unferth, if you were truly
> as keen or courageous as you claim to be
> Grendel would never have got away with
> such unchecked atrocity, attacks on your king,
> havoc in Heorot and horrors everywhere.

But he knows he need never be in dread
of your blade making a mizzle of his blood
or of vengeance arriving ever from this quarter—
from the Victory-Shieldings, the shoulderers of the spear.

—·—·—·—·—·—·—·—

This reasoned and forceful retort silences Unferth and gives the Danes hope. They see a Beowulf that, as Hrothgar will later describe him, is "even-tempered, prudent and resolute." These are uncommon qualities and the Danes are impressed. Here is Hrothgar's full speech:

—·—·—·—·—·—·—·—

Beowulf, my friend,
your fame has gone far and wide,
you are known everywhere. In all things you are
    even-tempered,
prudent and resolute. So I stand firm by the promise of
    friendship
we exchanged before. Forever you will be
your people's mainstay and your own warriors'
helping hand.

—·—·—·—·—·—·—·—

Will such an approach work? Can we get our Unferths to back down if we are even-tempered, prudent, and resolute? For a recent instance of someone battling with American resentment, let's turn to President Obama. This is where the tone is set for the country as a whole, and we can take the lessons learned from the president's efforts and apply them to how we deal with resentment in our own communities.

Almost from his first day in the White House, Obama encountered Unferth-like taunts, and throughout his term he has been targeted by Grendelian resentment at a level unseen by any previous occupant of the White House. As *Washington Post* columnist

Colbert King noted in a February 2012 column on "the demonizing of Barack Obama," in this election year "there is no invective too repugnant, too vicious to throw at this president of the United States." Nor has any president since Abraham Lincoln seen his legitimacy so questioned, whether it was legislators refusing to discourage (and sometimes even embracing) absurd conspiracies about Obama's birth; a House representative shouting "You lie" in a presidential address; or Republican House and Senate members rebuffing White House invitations and, at one point, the president's request to speak before Congress. The hue and cry about voter fraud in a number of states, while unsupported by any evidence of actual fraud, appears to be spurred by the belief that Obama's election was somehow tainted—or at least that voting by unworthy Americans must be suppressed to prevent further Obamas.

In retrospect, we should have expected this would be the case with the first black president. American racism, described by William Faulkner as "that ancient subterrene atavistic ethnic fear," is behind the birther conspiracies, as well as the explosion of gun sales, the proliferation of white supremacist groups, and Rush Limbaugh's tirades. It may be the subtle subtext behind accusations that Obama is "the food stamp president" (Newt Gingrich) or "the entitlement president" (Mitt Romney), since the recipients of food stamp and welfare have historically—and inaccurately—been seen as mostly African American.

Obama's reluctance to respond to the attacks on himself and other targeted groups has been criticized by some on the American Left, who have wanted him to express their own rage and fight fire with fire. Liberal *New York Times* columnist Maureen Dowd sees the president as timid and spineless in domestic matters and has derided him as "Obambi."

Whether or not he should have more forcefully confronted Congress or the financial sector, there is nevertheless something to be said for the president's calm. Beowulf displays behavior comparable to Obama's and, early in his life, receives similar criticism.

In fact, the poem is so aware of the temptation to meet force with force that it tells us what young Beowulf does *not* do when confronted with attackers, whether human or monstrous. He does *not* give in to anger, instead staying calm and controlling both his rage and his strength:

—·—·—·—·—·—·—

[He] never cut down
a comrade who was drunk, kept his temper
and, warrior that he was, watched and controlled
his God-sent strength and his outstanding
natural powers.

—·—·—·—·—·—·—

Not sure what to make of such self-control, Beowulf's companions early on view him as a wimp, much as Dowd and other liberals have viewed Obama:

—·—·—·—·—·—·—

He had been poorly regarded
for a long time, was taken by the Geats
for less than he was worth: and their lord too
had never much esteemed him in the mead-hall.
They firmly believed that he lacked force,
that the prince was a weakling ...

—·—·—·—·—·—·—

Beowulf goes on to prove that calm self-control does not equal weakness, however. In fact, this very calm and self-control is central to his leadership, and eventually his critics come around. For instance, the young Beowulf is able to persuade a group of young warriors to join him on a risky sea voyage to King Hrothgar's kingdom. Perhaps we can view this as Obama's quest for the presidency, a journey that initially seemed Quixotic. Against formidable odds, he drew supporters with his vision of hope and change and, against all probability, made it to the White House.

Like Beowulf, Obama has taken a measured look at the monsters raging through the house and often responds with calm. "I like to know what I'm talking about before I speak," he said early in his presidency to a reporter who asked him why it had taken the administration a couple of days to express outrage after government-bailout beneficiary AIG awarded large executive bonuses. He appears to know which of the attacks against him are caused by the heady drink of political posturing and which should be taken seriously. When the monster of resentment thinks he is asleep and reaches out for him, he has proved good at counterattacking, turning perceived losses into victories.

Obama has also made an attempt to understand the resentment. Although his "cling to guns or religion" statement was otherwise a low point of his 2008 presidential campaign since it cast him as a patronizing elitist, it did show that he was trying to "grapple" with Grendelian anger. Noting that jobs in rural Pennsylvania and the Midwest "have been gone now for 25 years and nothing's replaced them," Obama went on to say that "each successive administration has said that somehow these communities are gonna regenerate and they have not. And it's not surprising then they get bitter, they cling to guns or religion or antipathy to people who aren't like them or anti-immigrant sentiment or anti-trade sentiment as a way to explain their frustrations."

Obama may have been taking a page from Thomas Frank's 2004 book *What's the Matter with Kansas: How Conservatives Won the Heart of America* in his comments. Frank argues that, feeling powerless, conservative Kansans act out their rage against cultural liberals, even though, in doing so, they accede to their own economic degradation. After all, they are filling the pockets of the wealthiest Americans, not their own, when they oppose the estate tax, labor unions, bank regulations, and progressive income taxes. Democrats, Frank believes, must stop condescendingly lecturing Middle America about its reactionary values, cut their own ties with big money, and begin to address class inequity. If they do, he thinks, they will convince Kansans to return to their fundamental decency—and vote Democratic. Frank believes that most of them have not been rendered so monstrous by rage that they are impervious to outreach. On the contrary, they can and should be appealed to.

Obama, however, has had difficulties with rhetorical outreach. While Beowulf seems a man of the people, Obama too often comes across as a cerebral technocrat and doesn't do well rallying his troops (the American public) to his side. Unlike Beowulf, he has not convinced them of his strengths nor exposed the deficiencies of his adversaries (although an improving economy would help in both instances). Nor has Obama maintained control of his narrative, which has allowed our American Unferths to come up with their own versions of the facts. As a result, the Grendel archetype of resentful destruction has not torn itself free from Obama's enemies but rather has grown in confidence, possessing them all the more. The president has consequently been on the defensive, seeing his dreams of change slashed and devoured.

The Republican Party has its own version of the problem and has allowed Grendelian anger to turn it into a band of Unferths. This has been of great concern to moderate conservatives like *New York Times* columnist David Brooks, who points out that Republican leaders are to blame for the way the party's extreme right prolonged the nomination battle and pulled probable nominee Mitt Romney increasingly away from the center, which is where national elections are historically won. As Brooks rhetorically asks,

> where have these party leaders been over the past five years, when all the forces that distort the G.O.P. were metastasizing? Where were they during the rise of Sarah Palin and Glenn Beck? Where were they when Arizona passed its beyond-the-fringe immigration law? Where were they in the summer of 2011 when the House Republicans rejected even the possibility of budget compromise?

What Brooks would like to see is his party's leaders acting more like Beowulf:

> The wingers call their Republican opponents RINOs, or Republican In Name Only. But that's an insult to the rhino, which is a tough, noble beast. If RINOs were like rhinos, they'd stand up to those who seek to destroy them. Actually, what the country needs is some real Rhino Republicans. But the professional Republicans never do that. They're not rhinos. They're Opossum Republicans. They tremble for a few seconds then slip into an involuntary coma every time they're challenged aggressively from the right.
>
> Without real opposition, the wingers go from strength to strength.

Brooks is good at seeing how anger feeds on trembling opposition. He doesn't acknowledge, however, that moral cowardice is not the only force at play. The Republicans have benefited, at least in the short term, from using Grendelian anger as a weapon, halting Obama's agenda and insuring them success in the 2010 elections. That's why many who knew better tacitly encouraged "birther" conspiracy theories or at least did not forthrightly condemn them. In some ways these Republican leaders have been like King Hrothgar, who might decry the violence that has broken out in his hall but who still gives a known fratricide like Unferth a place of honor at his feet.

Our own blustering Unferths may be more pawns than instigators in a subtle power game. While Unferth loses his audience and falls silent following Beowulf's strong rhetorical display, it's probably naïve to think that Obama or possum Republicans would have prevailed had they only defended their principles more forcefully. Rhetoric doesn't really work on those who are making cold-blooded calculations. That is why I am interested in the subplot involving Regent Hrothulf, even though he is a minor figure in the epic. Hrothulf is the man charged with safeguarding Hrothgar's sons should the king die early. Like the cynical power-mongers of the Republican Party, he will prove impervious to attempts at conciliation. He therefore serves as a useful example for how to handle our own calculating resenters.

DEALING FORCEFULLY WITH A MURDEROUS SCHEMER

Like the current leaders of the Republican Party, Hrothulf believes that he should rule the kingdom and will stop at nothing to achieve his goal. When King Hrothgar dies, Hrothulf kills Hrothgar's eldest son and takes control of Denmark. In other words, he doesn't play fair but, driven by resentment and envy, contravenes the political rules of his time and makes a naked power grab.

The Hrothulf episode reminds us to be smart when we deal with monstrous resentment. We must rigorously assess each individual who has been possessed by Grendelian anger and respond in ways that are effective. The poem likewise warns us to be suspicious of naïve idealists who think everyone will get along. In Anglo-Saxon society, naïve idealists got killed. King Hrothgar's wife, the Danish Queen Wealtheow, is one of these naïfs and so provides us with a cautionary tale.

While King Hrothgar is still alive, both he and his queen know they must be wary of Hrothulf. (We never see Hrothulf directly in the poem but we can tease out a number of facts about him from the queen's words and from oblique references.) King Hrothgar is worried enough about a potential power grab from Hrothulf or someone like him that he even contemplates making Beowulf his heir, an option he probably wouldn't consider if he were convinced that his succession, in the event of his early death, would go smoothly.

Beowulf as Danish king, however, would no more bring an instant end to hyperpartisanship than Obama has. If Beowulf were suddenly named as successor, Grendelian resentment probably would arise in three individuals: Hrothulf and the two legitimate heirs to the throne, Hrothgar's sons. Nor is Queen Wealtheow pleased by the prospect of her sons being disinherited. She therefore advises a conciliatory approach for dealing with Hrothulf and the threat he poses to a legitimate succession. Under the guise of pouring wine and bestowing gifts, she engages in subtle diplomacy to placate Hrothgar. Her goal is to keep Hrothgar from naming Beowulf as his heir, ensuring that her sons will inherit the throne.

Here are the steps she takes when dealing with her husband:

⫸ she names her fear and acknowledges Hrothgar's, telling the king that she has heard the rumors that he wants to name Beowulf his heir. Perhaps this is meant to shame him and remind him of his duty to his own sons;

⫸ shame is not enough to allay deep fear, however, so she backs up her statement of the problem by reassuring Hrothgar that his nephew Hrothulf will take good care of their sons should anything happen to the king. These words are aimed at Hrothulf as well at Hrothgar. She is reminding the nephew of his uncle's past favors to him, hoping that she has found a way to shame him, too, into behaving properly.

Of course, she also wants to keep Beowulf from accepting any regency offers. Therefore:

⫸ she speaks to Beowulf's higher nature, asking him to be a shield to her sons. Maybe she even hopes that he will protect them against Hrothulf;

⫸ she bestows lavish gifts on Beowulf, trying to create a sense of good will and obligation.

As it happens, Queen Wealtheow's reassurances to Hrothgar prove to be spectacularly wrong, something that should be borne in mind as we watch the president negotiating with radical Republicans in the House. After Hrothgar dies, Hrothulf will ignore the loyalty and gratitude that Wealtheow had been counting on. Instead, much like the power-hungry leaders of our own

Republican Party he goes for the throne, setting off a civil war in the process. The poem makes clear that Wealtheow's naïve, idealistic attempts at diplomacy are worse than useless. Rather than bringing about the "bipartisan" peace she seeks, she only creates the conditions for her children to be killed and her kingdom to be taken over by an ambitious villain.

Many on the left have criticized Obama for exhibiting a similar naïveté. They complain that his assumption that Republicans would bargain in good faith and be open to compromise has led him to "give away the store" in one negotiation after another. Indeed, the nadir of Obama's presidency may have come in the summer of 2011 when radical House Republicans were refusing to raise the debt ceiling, thereby threatening to send the country into credit default and possibly a second recession. Seeking a "grand bargain," Obama went into private negotiation with Republican Speaker of the House John Boehner, only to be (in his words) "left at the altar" when Boehner reneged. Although Obama had taken a diplomatic gamble, infuriating Democrats and Keynesian economists with his $4 of budget reduction for every $1 in tax hikes, Tea Party Republicans were furious with Boehner for not scrubbing *every* tax hike from the deal. In the end, both parties punted any final decisions to after the 2012 election, and Obama's popularity ratings plummeted.

The *Beowulf* poet could have foreseen this end. The Wealtheow incident in the poem makes it clear how pointless it is to negotiate with monstrous anger since such anger is by definition closed to reason. In Anglo-Saxon times, a settlement between warring parties could take the form of blood money, but Grendel, we are told, refuses to make such deals:

—·—·—·—·—·—·—·—

> [He] would never
> parley or make peace with any Dane
> nor stop his death-dealing nor pay the death-price.

—·—·—·—·—·—·—·—

Under the influence of the Tea Party, the Republican Party shows a similar refusal to parley and make peace. *Beowulf* teaches us to identify those who will not play by the rules and act accordingly. Dealing with them can be different than dealing with petty resenters like Unferth, who can sometimes be shamed into good behavior.

THE POWER OF MORAL AUTHORITY

Before entirely dismissing Obama as a weak Queen Wealtheow, however, we should note that some key commentators have defended Obama's approach. In his much-quoted *Newsweek* article "How Obama's Long Game Will Outsmart His Critics," Andrew Sullivan makes the case that Obama is not afraid to compromise even when it makes him appear weak, figuring that even rejection may help his long-term goals. In this framing of the conflict, Grendel may initially think he has a free shot at sleeping Geat warriors, but Beowulf grabs him the moment he overreaches.

A related argument, flagged by Sullivan, is made by one "Tom," an anonymous on-line respondent to a *Washington Monthly* column in the fall of 2011. Tom sees Obama operating out of the non-violence tradition of the Civil Rights movement:

> Obama acts entirely within the tradition of mainstream African American political strategy and tactics. The epitome of that tradition was the non-violence of the Civil Rights Movement, but [it] goes back much further in time. It recognizes the inequality of power between whites and blacks. Number one: maintain your dignity. Number two: call your adversaries to the highest principles they hold. Number three: Seize the moral high ground and Number four: Win by winning over your adversaries, by revealing the contradiction between their own

ideals and their actions. It is one way that an
oppressed people struggle (qtd. in Sullivan, "Civil
Rights Prism").

Tom works under the assumption that ultimately enough
decent Americans will rally to the moral high ground. He might
have in mind Martin Luther King's "the arc of history bends
towards justice," a quotation that Obama has repeated. In this
regard, we should recall that Wealtheow is not a complete failure
in her appeal to "highest principles." She is partially successful
for a short time at least, persuading Hrothgar not to dispossess his
son, thereby giving her some latitude. Beowulf appears to learn
from her as well. When he returns to Geatland and eventually
becomes a regent himself, it may be because of Wealtheow's influence that he acts as a regent should.

Through the story of Beowulf's regency, the poem shows why
it is good for societies to follow established rules. After Beowulf's
king dies, the queen offers him the throne, potentially dispossess-
ing her young son Heardred. Beowulf, however, refuses to become
king. Instead, he serves the boy and guards the kingdom for him.
He does eventually become king, but only after Heardred dies in
battle. What the poem says about Beowulf's decision should be
adopted as a guide for how Americans engage in politics:

—·—·—·—·—·—·—·—

So ought a kinsman act,
instead of plotting and planning in secret
to bring people to grief, or conspiring to arrange
the death of comrades.

—·—·—·—·—·—·—·—

Because Beowulf puts his country over ego, Geatland experiences a peaceful succession. Grendelian rage never establishes a
foothold there.

FIRMNESS ALWAYS NECESSARY

Queen Wealtheow's mistake is in relying exclusively upon the extended hand of compromise and conciliation (although admittedly she doesn't have many options). Beowulf's struggle with Grendel teaches us that conciliatory gestures must be supplemented with a firm grip. In the 2011 summer debacle, Obama may not have squeezed hard enough. Learning from one's mistakes is always the test of a leader, so it will be interesting to see, throughout the remainder of 2012, how well Obama learns from his. He is certainly faring better since he began standing up to Republicans rather than attempting to please them. On a couple of occasions when he has responded to Republican intransigence with firmness of his own, the opposition has backed down.

For instance, in January of 2012, despite impeachment threats, Obama made recess appointments to fill filibustered vacancies. Subsequently he has refused to offer meaningful concessions over extending the payroll tax cut, which he felt was necessary to keep the economy improving. In both cases he prevailed and his approval ratings have gone up.

Perhaps what Obama learned is that Americans respond to a leader who, while reasonable, also refuses to back down in the face of divisiveness. King Hrothgar and the Danes certainly admire such behavior:

—————————————

[F]ar-famed in battle, the prince of Bright-Danes
and keeper of his people counted on Beowulf,
on the warrior's steadfastness and his word.
So the laughter started, the din got louder
and the crowd was happy.

—————————————

In figuring out how to handle the American electorate, perhaps

Obama should divide it up into Beowulfs, Unferths and Hrothulfs. The Beowulfs can be counted on to put their country first and will be selfless and do the right thing. The Unferths, despite their complaining, can be brought around with a firm approach, especially if those around them are also convinced. The Hrothulfs, however, cannot be reached; instead, they require shows of strength and constant vigilance. A successful leader must make accurate assessments and figure out which opponents respond to a handshake and which to a firm grip. When leaders assess correctly, as Beowulf does with Unferth, they carry the day. When they misread the situation, as Queen Wealtheow does with Hrothulf, they pay a fatal price.

BATTLING AT THE LOCAL LEVEL

I have been focusing on President Obama and the Republican leadership, but since a democracy is only as strong as its citizens, let's look at how we confront resentment on a local level. A combination of extended hand and firm grip has led to one of the most remarkable shifts of the past twenty years, America's increasing acceptance of homosexuality. This attitudinal shift has been reflected in the repeal of the military's "Don't Ask, Don't Tell" policy and in the passage of laws in a handful of states allowing same-sex marriage.

The change is due in large part to gays and lesbians all over the country summoning up a courage that I would describe as warrior-like and coming out to friends and families. Talking the language of love, they have extended hands, but they have also shown themselves to be resolute and firm. This approach has often encouraged those who know them to step out of their own monstrous prejudices and into acceptance. Confronted with this combination of love and resolve, the monster of homophobia has blinked.

We've seen similar victories in other areas from those combin-

ing outreach with determination. Ohio voters, responding posi-
tively to arguments of basic fairness, restored bargaining rights to
public employees, which had been stripped from them by the gov-
ernor and state legislature. Arizona voters acted out of a similar
sense of basic decency when they removed from office Arizona
Senate President Russell Pearce, author of a particularly virulent
anti-immigration law. Occupy Wall Street challenged decades-long
rifts between blue and white-collar workers by focusing on their
common suffering. And let's not forget that the entire nation
elected a black president in 2008.

Granted, these battles are a long way from over and there will
always be Regent Hrothulfs who regard the kingdom as their
rightful possession and seek to exclude others. But whether we
find ourselves up against a Hrothulf, an Unferth, or some other
warrior who has been possessed by Grendelian resentment, we
must summon up heroic resolve, be smart, and resist the impulse
to lash out.

That is what it means to be a Beowulf. When we encounter fellow Americans whose humanity has been momentarily stripped
away, it is understandable why we would be tempted to grab our
verbal swords and start flailing away. After all, an individual possessed by a monstrous rage can seem preternaturally powerful and
perhaps, like Grendel, appear to stand ten feet tall. But an angry
response is ultimately ineffective as our anger only feeds the monster. People harden over when they are self-righteously denounced
for their homophobia or racism.

This, then, is our challenge: we are to assess the attacks and
the people who propagate them, and then we must insert ourselves
resolutely but also intelligently into the battle. And we are not to
lose hope. When tolerance battles with resentment, we must
believe in the grip powered by respect and conviction rather than
in the rending and tearing fueled by fear.

We may not reach everyone. The Regent Hrothulfs of the
world will always be looking to attack when our defenses are
down. But—as the marriage equality movement has done, and the

voters in Ohio and Arizona—we can assist at least some of our antagonists to discover "the better angels of [their] nature." The phrase, of course, is Lincoln's, who understood something about resentment. All we need is a working majority.

Chapter 3

GRENDEL'S MOTHER: DESTRUCTIVE GRIEF

On a cold November election eve in Chicago's Grant Park, Barack Obama stood before 65,000 supporters and an international television audience and declared that the American dream had just been reaffirmed. "If there is anyone out there who still doubts that America is a place where all things are possible," he said, "who still wonders if the dream of our founders is alive in our time, who still questions the power of our democracy, tonight is your answer."

The speech concluded in the same vein. "This is the time," America's new young president said, "to reclaim the American dream and reaffirm that fundamental truth, that, out of many, we are one; that while we breathe, we hope. And where we are met with cynicism and doubts and those who tell us that we can't, we will respond with that timeless creed that sums up the spirit of a people: Yes, we can!"

Obama's supporters, and even some who had voted against him, went to bed that night believing (as the more enthusiastic put it) that we had entered a new "post-racial" America and that the old forces of resentment and division were dead. Few realized that Grendelian resentment has a mother. They awoke from their beautiful dream a few months later to find a new type of monster raging through the hall and prepared to sacrifice everything, even the country itself, in her fury.

Of course, that's not how the extreme Right saw it. For them, the American Dream had been hijacked and Obama himself represented the greatest threat to it. Their dream did not include a Kenyan-American as president. Nor did it include an ever-expanding Hispanic population and a growing number of American Muslims. Nor did it include men marrying men, women marrying women, and gays and lesbians serving openly in the military. Nor did it include an America weakened by two prolonged wars whose leaders, rather than brandishing their military might, engaged quietly and cautiously in nuanced diplomacy. Of course, disappearing jobs and ravaged retirement accounts played a role in the dissatisfaction, turning up the heat and undercutting many people's receptiveness to the new faces that were claiming a piece of the pie.

The grievers invoked first principles as they vented their rage. They spoke of the Boston Tea Party, the Founding Fathers, the Constitution, even (in the case of Michele Bachmann) a pre-Civil War South that was supposedly better for Black families than the present. Actual historical facts did not matter—these mad-as-hell bereaved citizens were mourning because, as they saw it, the most precious part of their country had been destroyed, along with their dreams.

A YouTube clip from the angry Tea Party summer of 2009 captures some of this anger and hurt. A middle-aged woman, standing at the back of a raucous town meeting, is shaking hysterically and crying. Barely able to speak through her tears, she moans, "I have never seen my America turned into what it has turned into, and I want my America back."

Such outsized displays of angry grief have had a disproportionate political impact. Republican legislators concluded that they had the backing they needed to do anything they could to stop the president, including pushing American politics to the breaking point.

Meanwhile Democrats, caught off guard by a fury that did not appear willing to negotiate, became demoralized and defensive. It didn't help that they had their own disillusioned dreamers, some of whom raged against the Tea Party, some of whom inveighed against Obama's apparent betrayal of progressive issues, some of whom sank into depression. The energy was with the Right and, in the off-year elections of 2010, Republicans retook the House, made inroads in the Senate, and seized governorships and state legislatures around the country.

In short, America has a grieving problem. Some of the grievers are tearing the hall apart, and those who should be standing up to them are wrestling with their own sorrow. It's as though there's a sibling fight with no adult in the room. One sibling is hysterical at the state of the house (it's not like the luxurious mansion next door) and is throwing a temper tantrum while the other, who believes in acting responsibly, feels overwhelmed and at a loss and doesn't know how to convince the outraged one to engage in collective problem-solving. And no, the solution is not to beat up on your smaller brothers and sisters.

Beowulf once again sails to the rescue, giving us images and stories that allow us to examine that angry grief up close. By watching the steps that Beowulf undertakes to defeat Grendel's Mother, we learn how we ourselves can handle the destructive sorrow that eats away at our country.

AMERICA'S GRIEF PROBLEM

The crying woman on television was grieving the symbolic death of her American dream whereas it was the actual slaughter of friends that would have set Anglo-Saxon warriors to grieving. For the original audience of the *Beowulf* epic, the sequence of monsters in the poem would have been grimly logical: a warrior, in the fury of resentment, plunges his sword into a fellow warrior. This might temporarily assuage his own inner monster—his envy and resentment—but it unleashes vengeful grief, an even darker monster. The murdered man's relatives, male and female, become possessed by Grendel's Mother and embark on a blood feud.

In the poem we see accounts of such blood feuds, with vendetta answering vendetta. At the end of his life Beowulf looks back over his life and notes that vendettas have deprived him of his three predecessors and that his people, the Geats, have in turn exacted their own revenge on those who attacked them, creating a seemingly endless cycle of violence and loss. We see many such feuds in the world today.

The United States may not be marked by the physically violent feuds of the Middle East, Somalia, or the Congo, but angry grieving still burns hot over what psychologists call symbolic or psychosocial loss. The loss of a dream, a hope, or a cherished image can cut as deeply as a more tangible loss and helps explain much of the emotional turbulence we have been witnessing.

Beowulf elucidates the connection between grief and resentment by pairing those two monsters, making resentful Grendel the son of Grendel's grieving mother. We too can see how the grief resulting from the perceived loss of America's economic dream would give birth to resentment, how it would lead some citizens to blame, envy, and denounce others. More than anything, Americans are embittered by a sense of unfairness. Given what we as Americans have been led to expect, the system seems stacked against us. When we rage against losing the dream, we open ourselves to possession by Grendel's Mother. When we resent others for seemingly having unfair access to that dream, we can turn into resentful Grendels.

A James Baldwin passage from *Notes of a Native Son* succinctly sums up the psychology if we substitute the word "resentment" for "hate" and the word "grief" for "pain." Baldwin writes, "I imagine one of the reasons people cling to their hates [resentments] so stubbornly is because they sense, once hate [resentment] is gone, they will be forced to deal with pain [grief]."

Pained grieving wants someone to pay just as much as resentment-driven hate does. It matters little to Grendel's Mother that her son brought his disaster upon himself. A rightwing mourner is not going to dwell on the fact that, say, the economy tanked under the Republicans, not the Democrats, or that the rampant greed of wealthy financiers and large corporations was far more to blame than the shenanigans of illegal immigrants and welfare freeloaders. Indeed, rightwing rage might burn even hotter to repress the knowledge that those in whom they put their trust were actually at fault.

When you are grieving, it also doesn't matter who pays: your target—your scapegoat—doesn't have to be the actual person who killed your dream. You just have to make *someone* experience all the pain that is overwhelming you. Although Beowulf is the one who killed Grendel, Grendel's Mother achieves payback by slaying not Beowulf and not even King Hrothgar, whose lack of favor towards Grendel provoked the resentment in the first place. Instead she kills Aeschere, King Hrothgar's best friend.

The poem makes clear that attacks are only one way that grievers express their angry sorrow. They can also sink deep within themselves. Many Americans today are in a silent state of enraged despair about their country. The lake where Grendel's Mother resides provides us with a comprehensive picture of America's emotional state: sometimes the monster broods sullenly in the depths, sometimes she emerges to vent her rage.

PARALYZED WITH GRIEF

The brooding of Grendel's Mother is captured in the lake's frigid waters. The poet tells us that the lake is located in a "frost stiffened wood" and is fed by cold mountain streams. To a casual observer the lake appears cold and impassive. Anger is still there, however. We just can't see it because it lurks beneath the surface.

Sigmund Freud famously said that secrets make us sick, and this lake represents one sick mind. Sea creatures writhe in its depths. We see the rage only when the sun goes down, at which point "a dirty surge is pitched towards the heavens." For the Anglo-Saxons, the lake would have been a powerful metaphor for the mind of a warrior who has lost a comrade and who is pushing his feelings under for fear that they will engulf him. We may hide our emotions from others and even from ourselves, but they are nevertheless alive, and they come out into the open when our defenses are down (say, in our nightmares).

Just as Unferth and Regent Hrothulf were instances of how hot and cold resentment enter a warrior and turn him into a monster, so the poem gives us some characters who are invaded by the Mother's hot grief and others by her cold misery. They become either angry ragers or paralyzed mourners. King Hrothgar is a paralyzed mourner.

When the king loses Aeschere, he falls into a deep depression and is prepared to give up. In king-centered societies, such behavior by a leader would have left the kingdom directionless, damaging it almost as much as a king who lashed out. Today in the United States, dispirited leaders and demoralized citizens eat away at our can-do spirit.

Beowulf manages to get Hrothgar moving again by encouraging him to seek revenge (in other words, moving him from a cold version of grief to a hot version). But in yet another subplot, the poem also gives us an instance of a king who sinks so deeply into the monster-filled lake of his mind that he never emerges. The story of Hrethel, Beowulf's grandfather, is one of the saddest in the poem and shows us why depression is a severe problem for societies.

When Hrethel's eldest son is accidentally killed by his second son, probably in a hunting accident, all the joy goes out of Hrethel's life. The poem compares the bereaved father to someone whose son has been legally executed and who therefore has no outlet for his rage. The poet's description of Hrethel losing all interest in life and crawling into bed is heartrending:

—·—·—·—·—·—·—·—

The wisdom of age is worthless to him.
Morning after morning, he wakes to remember
that his child is gone; he has no interest
in living on until another heir
is born in the hall, now that his first-born

has entered death's dominion forever.
He gazes sorrowfully at his son's dwelling,
the banquet hall bereft of all delight,
the windswept hearthstone; the horsemen are sleeping,
the warriors under ground; what was is no more.
No tunes from the harp, no cheer raised in the yard.
Alone with his longing, he lies down on his bed
and sings a lament; everything seems too large,
the steadings and the fields.

—·—·—·—·—·—·—

This is the mind of those Americans who find themselves at the bottom of a black slough of despond. They lack the will to move on and stew in numbed silence. They don't even show up at Tea Party rallies. Instead they opt out of the political process altogether or perhaps become easy prey for even more demagogic leaders.

HOT REVENGE

In contrast to Hrothgar and Hrethel, the poem has a character who, while at first frozen, later breaks out into bloody flame. Through the story of Hengest's revenge against Finn, we see what happens when Grendel's Mother enters our fellow citizens and provokes them to attack.

The Finn subplot is convoluted and confusing but it vividly captures the mourner's thirst for vengeance. Denmark and Friesland try to patch up a feud through a diplomatic alliance, marrying the Danish king's daughter Hildeburh to the Frisian king Finn. Unfortunately, the marriage is no more effective than a handshake between President Obama and the Republican Speaker of the House, and fighting breaks out again. In the battle, Queen Hildeburh loses both her Danish brother and her Frisian son. Only her younger brother Hengest survives.

As neither the Danes nor the Frisians triumph, the two sides must live together in Finn's household in an uneasy truce. Think of them as Democrats and Republicans trying to make nice while President Finn works on maintaining the peace. Finn does everything in his power to prevent more fighting, including allocating separate quarters for the Danes and doling out gifts equally to both sides. He also bans, under pain of death, all taunting and other hate speech that could rekindle the hostilities:

—·—·—·—·—·—·—

So if any Frisian
                    stirred up bad blood
with insinuations
                    or taunts about this,
the blade of the sword
                    would arbitrate it.

—·—·—·—·—·—·—

Imagine you are brother Hengest—or, for that matter, a Tea Partier still furious about Obama's election. In the immediate aftermath of the battle/election your anger, like the North Sea, is "shackled in ice." Blood-sullen, you are in a state of frozen anger:

—·—·—·—·—·—·—

                    Hengest stayed,
lived out that whole
                    resentful, blood-sullen
winter with Finn,
                    homesick and helpless.
No ring-whorled prow
                    could up then
and away on the sea.
                    Wind and water
raged with storms,
                    wave and shingle
were shackled in ice . . .

—·—·—·—·—·—·—

When the season changes, however, the frozen anger trans-
forms into hot rage, and King Finn's bloody death seems
inevitable:

—·—·—·—·—·—·—·—

The wildness in them
had to brim over.
The hall ran red
with blood of enemies.

—·—·—·—·—·—·—·—

While the mourning King Hrethel is cold and the angry brother
Hengest is hot, it is possible for destructive grieving to run both
hot and cold in the same individual. People can begin by taking
their anger out on others and then become sullen and withdrawn.
Or like brother Hengest, they can simmer away for months before
volcanically exploding. I suspect that many Tea Partiers, mourning the loss of their American dream, silently raged for years under
the Bush presidency and only blew into active anger with a
Democratic president. In fact, one could argue that they raged
under President Carter, went into remission under President
Reagan, began emerging again under the moderate President H.
W. Bush (the Patrick Buchanan insurgency), went into a full-
throated roar under President Clinton, subsided under President
George W. Bush, and are now at it again, not only against Obama
but also (as indicated by rightwing resistance to nominating the
"inevitable" Mitt Romney) against the Republican establishment.

Given the intensity of this anger, ameliorative measures are not
enough. The *Beowulf* poet could have predicted that President
Obama's attempts to be even-handed would, like the concessions
of King Finn, come to naught, ending in the very destruction each
even-handed leader was trying to avoid. I'm not saying that the
extreme Right is filled with Hengests who want to see the White
House running with Obama's blood, although extremists like television pundit Glen Beck and *Atlanta Jewish Times* owner

Andrew Adler have publicly fantasized about someone assassinating the president. Let's just say that many will experience a savage joy if he is defeated.

How do we respond to anger when it is this deep? How do we fight it in our fellow Americans and how, to be effective champions, do we overcome it in ourselves? The next chapter tells us how Beowulf approaches the problem.

Chapter 4

BEOWULF'S RESPONSE: FOUNDATIONAL VALUES

Grieving rage, whose archetype is Grendel's Mother, seems all but unstoppable when it possesses a fellow citizen. How do we deal with our raging compatriots— our sorrowing and revenge-obsessed Hengests —when, ignoring the protocols our King Finns have carefully set up to maintain civil order, they vent their rage on our vulnerable citizens? How do we rally our Hrothgars and our Hrethels when they descend into a funk and turn their backs on our problems?

Although this grieving has an economic cause, I have mentioned how the author of *What's the Matter with Kansas* regards the grievers as impervious to economic reasonableness. Rather, they seek scapegoats that are closer to hand and are more likely to vote against Obama, whose maternal grandparents were fellow middle class Kansans, than against "the guy who laid you off" (as one-time candidate Mike Huckabee has described Mitt Romney). If we are to penetrate their unhinged sorrow, we need something more than reason. We need some higher principle that we all share. We need some version of the great sword, forged by giant warriors in some past golden age, that Beowulf uses to slay Grendel's Mother.

AMERICA'S SWORD: THE AMERICAN DREAM

What is this sword? In Beowulf's case, it is the warrior ethos, which is at the heart of his society and at the core of his identity. He knows that, no matter how much grief is striking at his heart, he must stand strong.

The sword that most Americans share, even while otherwise in conflict, is a belief in fair play. We understand, as part of our DNA, that our one nation indivisible rests upon the principle that every individual deserves a fair shot at making something of his or her life. This is how we interpret the immortal assertion of the founding fathers that "all men are created equal, that they are endowed by their Creator with certain unalienable Rights, that among these are Life, Liberty and the pursuit of Happiness." The principle is so sacred to us—every morning as children we pledge allegiance to "liberty and justice for all"—that at critical moments we have been willing to put this larger ideal above our narrow, parochial interests.

That is why, sooner or later, most Americans have accepted, as fully participating citizens, those who were once excluded, whether they be non-property owners, Germans, Irish, African slaves, Indians, Italians, Poles, Chinese, Russian Jews, Catholics, Mormons, women, Hispanics, gays, lesbians, and others. Obviously, getting America to live up to that principle has sometimes required battles as fierce as Beowulf's struggle with Grendel's Mother. Sometimes, like Beowulf, we have stumbled. But because we see the cause as noble and just, we have been inspired to keep going. In a society where the wealthiest are gobbling up increasingly large slices of the collective pie, we can wield that sword on behalf of economic fairness.

Beowulf's example shows us both what we should and should not do to steer the conversation away from the fake issues that divide us and towards the real ones.

BEOWULF VS.
A GRIEVING MOTHER

After Grendel's Mother has attacked the mead hall and killed Aeschere, here's how Beowulf responds:

⋙→ first he notes that King Hrothgar's grief plunges him into deep despair. The country is in a depressed state, and Beowulf must model an alternative way of dealing with grief if it is to be preserved;

⋙→ he therefore journeys to the lake where she dwells and jumps in. The lake, a metaphor for the grieving mind, is a fearsome place. We have to face up to feelings of loss, both those of angry grievers and our own, if we want to save America;

⋙→ descending to the bottom of the lake (i.e., the depths of despair), Beowulf is captured by Grendel's Mother. The fear here is that, if we acknowledge our disappointment and grief, we will be swallowed up by these emotions and will never emerge;

⋙→ at first he attempts to use the sword that Unferth has given him to fight Grendel's Mother. As we saw with Grendel, an angry sword response doesn't work against angry grievers;

⋙→ then he attempts to use his extended hand and firm grip, which proved effective against Grendel. Grief goes deeper than resentment, however, and proves resistant to determined resolve;

⋙→ Grendel's Mother gets astride Beowulf and stabs at his chest with a knife. His heart is close to breaking and angry grieving threatens to take over;

⋙→ at this point he finds a gigantic sword that he didn't know was there. This he uses to slay Grendel's Mother and then, afterwards, to behead the corpse of Grendel, who is lying near by. America's founding principles ultimately prove more powerful than grief and resentment;

⋙→ a great light appears and the lake is cleansed of its monsters. This is what it feels like for a nation to rediscover hope.

The sword of economic and political fair play is not easy to wield since angry grieving, whether in its vengeful or its depressed form, is a formidable foe. Our grieving compatriots stand in the way of meaningful progress, and often we ourselves are not in the best mental state to stand up to them. Fortunately our giant forebears, those who in the past spurred America to live up to its founding ideals and expand the electoral franchise, are there for inspiration. We must strive to become the swordsmen and women that they were.

To do so, however, rigorous training is necessary. Beowulf can serve as coach.

He is one of those tough coaches that won't allow us to moan or whine or feel sorry for ourselves. He becomes impatient if we blame our failures on the ferocity of the rage or wallow in our grief. When King Hrothgar, after losing his friend, cries out, "Rest, what is rest?" Beowulf instructs the Danish king to take action against Grendel's Mother: "So arise, my lord, and let us immediately set forth on the trail of this troll-dam."

What does it take to grapple with resentment's troll-dam, which is to say with the grief that has given birth to envy and divisiveness? What, in our present case, does it take to stand up to raging Tea Partiers hardened over by their sense of loss? Before all else, we must acknowledge our own grief. That is the significance of Beowulf leaping into the lake. He must get to the root of the sorrow within himself.

Acknowledging that we are grieving is no small challenge. We may not admit how much we mourn America's failures because we fear being overwhelmed by our disappointment. Better to feign stoic indifference, pretending not to care as much as we really do. Many Americans spend time and energy ignoring the rage, resorting to distractions to steer clear of all the grim developments.

The ancient Greek historian Plutarch tells a story about such stoicism. Plutarch seems to praise the hardening over, but the story reveals the price we pay. He relates that a Spartan boy once hid a stolen fox under his cloak and refused to reveal it to avoid being disgraced. Plutarch reports that the boy "suffered the animal to tear out his bowels with its teeth and claws, and died rather than have his theft detected" (263).

I cite the story because it illuminates a comparable one found in *Beowulf*. After describing the grief-crazed lake in which Grendel's Mother lives, the poem tells us that a deer fleeing from hounds would rather be torn apart on the shore than leap into the water. The lake inspires that kind of fear.

It's a horrific image. We may think we can close our eyes to our sorrow. We may think we can be cold like the water and pretend not to care about the diminishing expectations of all but the wealthiest Americans, or that we can hide from others and from ourselves the sharp-toothed grieving under our cloak. And maybe no one else can see it. The reality, however, is that our internal hounds or foxes are tearing our insides to shreds.

FACING UP TO THE PROBLEM

It takes courage to acknowledge how much we love America and how much we grieve what is happening to her—which is to say, to jump into the monster-infested lake. Equivalent instances of Beowulf's bravery include the addict acknowledging that he has a problem and checking into a treatment center or the depressed individual facing up to her condition and visiting a therapist. This first step does not itself cleanse the lake of its demons—once we face up to our sorrow we've still got to deal with it—but nothing can happen without that step.

As the poem describes it, it takes Beowulf the better part of the day to reach the bottom of the lake (to fully open up to his distress). When he gets there, the monster comes and seizes him. Seeing the hero in the monster's arms seems to confirm our greatest fear, that our feelings will overwhelm us so that we never emerge. We just knew that our grieving would crush us the moment we gave ourselves permission to hope again.

Beowulf is where he needs to be, however. No longer a passive deer on the shore, he is ready to take action.

The battle occurs in an underwater hall, metaphor for the

inmost self. Beowulf tries three different ways of dealing with the grief that assaults him, and the first two don't work. We learn a great deal from all three.

RESPONDING WITH ANGER

He first draws his sword and attacks the monster. Unferth has given him this sword so it is a weapon that has been wielded in fratricidal anger (although the poem doesn't make a point of this). Reactive rage is understandable and very human, but the sword proves no more effective than the swords that were used against Grendel. Grendel's Mother is unfazed.

One can illustrate its ineffectiveness by contrasting two different approaches to grief, America's response to the 9-11 attacks with Norway's response to the shooting rampage of Christian fascist Andrea Breivik that killed 69 youths. Most Americans, following the steps of Grendel's Mother, were determined to make someone pay and were prepared to countenance violence visited upon pretty much anyone. This included not only those who were behind the attacks (Bin Laden, sheltered by the Taliban in Afghanistan) but those who, while innocent of 9-11, had thumbed their noses at the United States (Iraqi dictator Saddam Hussein).

The reaction did not put an end to angry grieving. We may have defeated Al-Qaeda and the Afghani Taliban that sheltered them, but the anger has only grown. Many on the extreme Right continue to argue for torture and for suspending habeas corpus for terrorism suspects. Some call for attacks against Iran and direct vitriol against their fellow Americans. Fear and anger are making us a smaller society.

Contrast this with the state of Norway as Breivik goes to trial. According to Reuters News,

> [I]t is striking too what "July 22," as the attacks are commonly called in Norway, has not done. It has not made Norwegians more fearful of one another, or

triggered calls for tougher anti-terrorist measures. Instead, many Norwegians say it has reaffirmed their faith in a society they like to see as liberal, tolerant and egalitarian.

Because he is a hero, Beowulf comes to realize that his angry sword thrusts will not make a dint in grieving's armor or take him back to the world of the sun. In Anglo-Saxon times, a clear-headed observer would have known that, when angry sorrow turns to violence, further grieving and interminable blood feuds are the result. In our own divisive politics, lashing out at grieving Americans who are lashing out at us only means that all of us become firmly mired in the dark lake. Grendel's Mother wants to hold us all permanently in thrall. Beowulf learns from his mistake and turns to a second approach.

RESPONDING WITH FIRM DETERMINATION

In the chapter on battling Grendel, I talked about the importance of understanding why our fellow Americans experience resentment. I argued that if we combine empathy (an extended hand) with firmness (a firm grip), we have a chance of penetrating their hardness and appealing to a common decency and sense of fair play. The same is true here only the hardness is more difficult to handle as sorrow goes deeper than resentment. That's why, when Beowulf tries to arm wrestle with the mother as he did with the son, he finds himself stumbling. The monster throws him, kneels upon his chest, and begins stabbing at his chest.

Put in terms of our situation, it is not enough for progressives or for President Obama to be calm and rational when dealing with enraged Tea Partiers. For that matter, it won't help them when they wrestle with their own grief. Unless they tap into a higher ideal, they will not penetrate the hardness of the one nor be able to maintain their own strength indefinitely. Sooner or later, like

Beowulf, we will falter and find Grendel's Mother sitting astride us, plunging her knife against the chest armor that guards the heart. Sooner or later, just as we feared, we will find ourselves trapped deep in depression. This is why we were reluctant to jump into the lake in the first place. To open the heart is to see it get stomped on.

Looking ahead to the monster that is the subject of chapters five and six, at such moments we are in danger of becoming cranky, cynical dragons. Dragons are those who have either abandoned their idealism altogether or, like certain disillusioned leftists who have become angry rightwing ideologues, seen it become distorted beyond all recognition. (I have in mind such neoconservatives as Irving Kristol, Norman Podhoretz, David Horowitz, and Charles Krauthammer.) I fear for those current-day progressives who are bitterly disillusioned with an Obama who persuaded them to hope again.

RESPONDING WITH A TRUTH WE HOLD TO BE SELF EVIDENT

Our higher ideal, expressed in *The Declaration of Independence*, is bigger than our individual grievances and will fortify us, just as, in his darkest moment, Beowulf's great sword fortifies him. Those who came before, like the warrior giants who forged that weapon, can infuse us with their spirit and inspire us to push through our pain. Wielding the sword means acknowledging and claiming that we stand on their shoulders. We are fighting the good fight, one that the Founding Fathers began and that Abraham Lincoln, Susan B. Anthony, Martin Luther King, Harvey Milk, and a host of others continued, each working to insure that America honor its promise.

The sword is so powerful that it can slay both sorrow (Beowulf stabs Grendel's Mother) and resentment (he beheads the corpse of Grendel that lies close by). The sword can rid the lake of its monsters.

Obama spoke of his heroic forebears on election night, those persons both known and unknown who paved the way to his remarkable victory. Hundreds of millions, at home and abroad, felt the exhilaration of a country acting in accord with its deep ideals of fairness. The description of Beowulf's victory over Grendel's Mother captures these feelings through images of sunshine and spring. The blade (the sharp edge of pain) melts in the monsters' blood like hard winter ice in a spring thaw, and the dark cavern is filled with light. This is how it feels to step out of the cold darkness and into hope:

———·———·———·———·———·———

A light appeared and the place brightened
the way the sky does when heaven's candle
is shining clearly.

———·———·———·———·———·———

Tea Partiers are not entirely wrong when they look to America's revolutionary roots for guidance. They, no less than progressives, are searching for America's promise of fairness, and this common heritage has the potential to bring both sides together. Granted, the differences at times seem insurmountable—when enraged grieving fixates on scapegoats, it proves a very powerful troll—but we've seen giant forebears like Lincoln and King successfully change hearts and minds in the past. Not all angry citizens are impervious to Walt Whitman's celebration of a diverse nation that contains multitudes.

We share with our fellow citizens a set of national symbols that articulate the American Dream, symbols like the American flag, the "Star Spangled Banner," the Pledge of Allegiance, "America the Beautiful," and (Martin Luther King used this one in his "Dream" speech) "My Country 'tis of Thee." Each of these calls for us to reach beyond our tribal impulses and embrace an inclusive vision.

Some progressives shy away from these symbols because political mountebanks have turned them into clubs and used them to beat up those they disagree with. Daily we see politicians and pundits proving Samuel Johnson's dictum that patriotism is the last refuge of the scoundrel. These false patriots claim that those who disagree with them are not "real Americans" (Sarah Palin), that they "don't understand America" (Mitt Romney on Barack Obama), even that they "hate America" (Rush Limbaugh). But that just means they are defining America by their fear and anger, by what they are against rather than what the country is for. They are wielding contorted imitations of the great sword, not the great sword itself. If we let them define the symbols for us, we play into their hands and Grendel's Mother will tear our hearts out.

True warriors distinguish between a true sword and debased versions. Grasping the true sword restores Beowulf's fighting spirit. Lifting high the banner of fairness can help us regain our own spirit and find common cause with our fellow citizens. Collectively reclaiming our vision of America, we can make our way through the dark lake and back into the light.

It won't be easy, but when has heroism ever been easy? It's enough to know that the battle is worth it.

Chapter 5

THE DRAGON: CYNICISM AND DESPAIR

At one point in *Beowulf*, King Hrothgar looks back into the past and sings the praises of the exemplary King Sigemund. This legendary warrior, he says, killed a dragon, took possession of its treasure hoard, and proved to be "a fence round his fighters."

By way of contrast, Hrothgar then shifts to the bad King Heremod, whom he describes as "a burden, a source of anxiety to his own nobles." Later in the poem we are told that Heremod vented his rage against his comrades, cut himself off from his own kind, gave no more rings, and became "a pariah king."

I cite these two examples because, when a wealthy developed capitalist nation like the United States faces a deep recession, it can choose to either battle the dragon or become a dragon. The United States today can either take the generous, caring and protective Sigemund route or the cynical, hoarding, and self-isolating Heremod route.

Following standard Keynesian economics, it might choose to borrow money to stimulate the construction of infrastructure, prevent layoffs of teachers and public sector employees, support the unemployed, and take other measures that will jumpstart an economic recovery. This Sigemund approach—let's call his "fence round his fighters" a "social safety net"—is intended to get the country through tough times. Once treasure is flowing again and employment is back up (so Keynesians tells us), the government can then pay back the deficit it ran up.

Or a country like ours might take a page out of King Heremod's book and refuse to give any more rings, enacting stringent austerity measures instead. There are economic arguments to be made for a Heremond strategy, including the notion that letting companies feel the full force of the free market (economists call it "creative destruction") results in great efficiency, rooting out the weak and rewarding the strong. Furthermore, proponents say that deficit reduction tamps down the prospect of inflation while protecting the next generation from paying today's bills.

But even in the best of cases, austerity cuts generally hit the most vulnerable members of the population far harder than the wealthy. Often when a Heremod spirit reigns, there is raging against weaker comrades, and recently we have been seeing pensioners, union members, government workers, and Medicaid and food stamp recipients blamed for our economic mess.

To cite one instance of a dragon-like austerity measure, in 2011, when unemployment was close to 10 percent, the Republican-led House of Representatives passed Paul Ryan's budget plan, which would have moved Medicare to a voucher program (thereby raising costs for beneficiaries), cut funds to education and food stamps, and trimmed Head Start and college Pell grants. At the same time, it called for abolishing the estate tax on multimillion-dollar estates and extending the top-end Bush tax cuts.

To show that it was serious, it again passed a similar budget in March 2012 that, according to Robert Greenstein, president of the respected Center of Budget and Policy Priorities, "would likely produce the largest redistribution of income from the bottom to the top in modern U.S. history and likely increase poverty and inequality more than any other budget in recent times (and possibly in the nation's history)." The plan has been embraced by Mitt Romney, who earlier in the year stated, "I don't care about the poor" in a pronouncement designed to trigger middle-class resentment against beneficiaries of what he calls Obama's "entitlement society."

Dragon gloom descends upon a society in which the upper class has sucked up most of the wealth, leaving everyone else to squabble about the remains. The engine that drives America has always been its belief that all of its citizens have a shot at participating in its wealth. When that belief begins to sputter, there is no glorious common future—only individual success stories—and the prevailing emotion becomes cynical despair.

Cynicism is a monstrous and deadening attitude that leaves a country feeling that it cannot solve the challenges that threaten it. In the midst of the Great Depression, America may have collectively rallied to the words of Franklin D. Roosevelt's second inaugural, "The only thing we have to fear is fear itself." Today, however, fear seems to be in the ascendency. President Obama's vision of lifting up those who are down is in danger of losing out to cynicism.

AMERICA IN THE DRAGON'S GRIP

Many participate in a country's dragonization. At the top there are those who game the system for their own private gain, using lobbyists to ensure that they receive special subsidies and tax loopholes. Then there are the legislators and media figures who benefit from their relationship with the economic elite, either financially or from the ego boost that comes with associating with power. Finally there are those who, while taking a financial pounding themselves, are willing to support the dragon system, turning their resentment and sorrow away from those who profit and towards other dragon victims.

Just as resentment and angry grieving have a cold and a hot side, so does dragon cynicism. In its cold state, a country in the dragon's grip gives up on a belief in collective solutions, including government solutions. Instead, it hunkers down and guards its possessions. When people have lost hope in a future, then the status quo prevails and the society becomes old, scaly-hard, and poisonous. In the case of the Republican Party, it is also becoming increasingly old and white. There is the deadly coldness of sclerosis and paralysis in a dragon society, and as long as no one disturbs existing wealth and power arrangements, the beast can seem to sleep.

If threatened by someone promising hope and change, however, the dragon turns fiery. In the poem, the dragon is roused when a thief sneaks in and steals a gold-plated cup. Wealthy Republicans saw Democrats trying to steal a cup in December 2011 when they proposed tax increases on those making over $250,000 to pay for extending a payroll tax break. Greeted with dragon fire, the Democrats promptly retreated. The poem captures the fierce anger of those who are dragon-possessed:

—··—··—··—··—··—

> The dragon began to belch out flames
> and burn bright homesteads; there was a hot glow
> that scared everyone, for the vile sky-winger
> would leave nothing alive in his wake.
> Everywhere the havoc he wrought was in evidence.
> Far and near, the Geat nation
> bore the brunt of his brutal assaults
> and virulent hate.

—··—··—··—··—··—

In recent American politics, dragon fire has sometimes taken the form of hyperbolic language, sometimes the form of corrosive legislation. The rightwing editorial pages of *The Wall Street Journal* regularly urge corporations to circle the wagons and stave off the "socialist" president. Various rightwing millionaires and billionaires have been funneling money to angry protest groups (as the billionaire Koch brothers have done with the Tea Party Movement) and pledging to donate record amounts of money to campaign Super Pacs that relentlessly launch negative ads. Their allies in Congress, meanwhile, filibuster presidential appointees in order to hamstring the National Labor Relations Board and the Consumer Financial Agency. As of this date it remains to be seen whether conservative Supreme Court justices rule will rule against the Obamacare mandate, thereby preventing millions of Americans from receiving health care.

In the next chapter I will lay out how Beowulf fights the dragon spirit that is laying waste to his country's future hopes. Here I let the poem show us how America has arrived at its current impasse.

A DANGEROUS SENSE OF ENTITLEMENT

It all begins with a sense of entitlement, with the moneyed interests feeling they deserve an ever bigger slice of the American pie. Their belief that they are entitled far surpasses that of the poor, accused by Romney of expecting handouts. Ironically, anxiety rather than contentment arises from the conservative elite's growing prosperity. The more they get, the more worried they are that (in the words of *New York Magazine* blogger Jonathan Chait) the "masses" will use their political power "to gang up on us and seize our wealth."

Chait arrived at his understanding while trying to figure out why Supreme Court rulings are increasingly favoring the wealthy. The Obama era, he says, appears to have "unleashed deep-rooted conservative fears of economic democracy":

> Conservatives have come to see the majority's threatening ability to shape economic policy not merely as an impediment but as a dire existential threat.

A similar sense of paranoia is captured in *Beowulf* when King Hrothgar describes the evolution of a greedy king. I quote the extended description in full because it brilliantly charts the psychological progression. Hrothgar begins by noting how the wealthy and the powerful have been blessed with "fulfillment and felicity on earth," and I have noted how, in recent American history, the upward movement of the country's wealth began in the 1980's. That's when tax rates began to go down and financial speculation increased. Treasures were heaped upon our men and women "of distinguished birth"—if not by God, then by a globalized economy and favorable legislation:

—.—.—.—.—.—.—

It is a great wonder
how Almighty God in His magnificence
favors our race with rank and scope
and the gift of wisdom; His sway is wide.
Sometimes He allows the mind of a man
of distinguished birth to follow its bent,
grants him fulfillment and felicity on earth
and forts to command in his own country
that the Heavenly Powers gave him in the past.
He permits him to lord it in many lands . . .

—.—.—.—.—.—.—

The first sign of trouble is when the king starts to take all these gifts as his due. He thinks he is rich because "the whole world conforms to his will," not because he is fortunate to have been born into a race (in our case, the United States) that has been graced "with rank and scope and the gift of wisdom":

—.—.—.—.—.—.—

. . . until the man in his unthinkingness
forgets that it will ever end for him.
He indulges his desires; illness and old age
mean nothing to him; his mind is untroubled
by envy or malice or the thought of enemies
with their hate-honed swords. The whole world
conforms to his will, he is kept from the worst . . .

—.—.—.—.—.—.—

Arrogance, and with it discontent, continues to grow. The passage notes the imperceptible gradualness of the change. Instead of seeing himself joined with the country in a common enterprise, the king gradually finds himself resenting others. The "devious promptings of the demon start" as he imagines them eyeing "his" possessions:

— · — · — · — · — · — · —

> . . . until an element of overweening
> enters him and takes hold
> while the soul's guard, its sentry, drowses,
> grown too distracted. A killer stalks him,
> an archer who draws a deadly bow.
> And then the man is hit in the heart,
> the arrow flies beneath his defenses,
> the devious promptings of the demon start.
> His old possessions seem paltry to him now.
> He covets and resents; dishonors custom
> and bestows no gold; and because of good things
> he ignores the shape of things to come.

— · — · — · — · — · — · —

In the end, the poem predicts, the king will reap what he has sown:

— · — · — · — · — · — · —

> Then finally the end arrives
> when the body he was lent collapses and falls
> prey to its death; ancestral possessions
> and the goods he hoarded are inherited by another
> who lets them go with a liberal hand.

— · — · — · — · — · — · —

With our own wealthy citizens and their political and media allies, what once would have been seen as munificent is now regarded as "paltry." It is now assumed, for instance, that CEOs should be paid hundreds of times what their employees make, that golden parachutes should be the norm, and that any attempts to redistribute the wealth—say, through increasing income tax rates—are an egregious infringement. They even seek to forestall, through their angry opposition to the estate tax, the poem's fantasy of their money being liberally redistributed when they die.

The poem doesn't tell us exactly what it means to covet, resent, dishonor and bestow no gold, but we can come up with our own contemporary examples. For instance, if we believe that basic fairness should prevail in America and that everyone should have equal opportunity to succeed, then legislators dishonor that spirit when, seduced by lobbying dollars, they write favorable legislation for big corporations and steer large contracts and generous subsidies their way. If Americans on both the Left and the Right were furious over the TARP bank bailout, necessary though it may have been, it was because they feared that once again they were being scammed.

STIFLING HOPE

Cynicism itself can become a deliberate tactic used by the cynical. If the populace concludes that hope is illusory, then they are more likely to let sleeping dragons lie. That is why those guardians of the existing financial order have been determined to stifle the extraordinary outburst of hope unleashed by Obama's election.

Among those dreaming of a brighter future were people who could not afford insurance, stressed homeowners who couldn't pay their mortgages, debt-burdened college students, recent graduates worried about jobs, poor and unemployed people needing food stamps and financial assistance, laid-off factory workers who saw their jobs shipped overseas, construction workers hit by the housing bust, teachers and government employees who stood to benefit from government spending, and others. Yet Republicans voted almost unanimously to block any measures that helped them out, with Fox News, Rush Limbaugh, Tea Party activists and others disciplining any Republican moderate who was tempted to stray. Democrats were barely able to pass even watered-down legislation regulating those financial institutions whose excesses led to the 2008 financial collapse, and since then the new rules have been under sustained Republican attack.

Many came to see Congress and the White House alike as inept, cynically reasoning that as a collective we can no longer fix what is wrong with ourselves and even concluding that government itself is the problem. Soon after Obama took office, Sarah Palin was able to mock, "How's that hopey-changey thing workin' out for ya?"

Entrenched interests may reap financial and political rewards for their tactics, but their country has become sour. An emblem for today's United States is "the last veteran," the man into whose ancestral hall Beowulf's dragon moves and takes up residence.

A CULTURE IN DESPAIR

The last veteran is the final remaining member of a "highborn race" that has died out. Looking back, he can remember the times when he joined with his fellows in heroic deeds. There were feasting warriors, stamping war steeds, soaring falcons, and harp music. This is the positive energy associated with building a vibrant society. Think of that highborn race as America during "the Great Prosperity of 1947-1975."

Now the good times seem to him forever gone, even though he himself is rich. Heartsick, he constructs a burial mound, piles up his worldly goods around him, and dies. (An ironic 1980s bumper sticker comes to mind: "He who dies with the most toys wins.") First, however, he looks back at his past glory and sings a lament:

Now, earth, hold what earls once held
and heroes can no more; it was mined from you first
by honorable men. My own people
have been ruined in war; one by one
they went down to death, looked their last
on sweet life in the hall. I am left with nobody

to bear a sword or to burnish plated goblets,
put a sheen on the cup. The companies have departed.
The hard helmet, hasped with gold,
will be stripped of its hoops; and the helmet-shiners
who should polish the metal of the war-mask sleeps;
the coat of mail that came through all fights,
through shield-collapse and cut of sword,
decays with the warrior. Nor may webbed mail
range far and wide on the warlord's back
beside his mustered troops. No trembling harp,
no tuned timber, no tumbling hawk
swerving through the hall, no swift horse
pawing the courtyard. Pillage and slaughter
have emptied the earth of entire peoples.

— . — . — . — . — . — . — . —

While the cynical self-absorption of the moneyed classes and their allies is not the result of military devastation, billionaire Warren Buffett notes that America too has been experiencing a battle. Responding to his fellow wealthy Americans when they were accusing Obama of waging class warfare, the third richest person in the world said, "There's class warfare, but it's my class, the rich class, that's making war, and we're winning." Buffett, who believes that taxes on people like himself should be raised, is one who understands that he has benefited from living in America and should therefore give back to the country that has nurtured him. But he is a rare exception. Like the last veteran, a country that no longer thinks of itself as embarked on a great collective enterprise falls into depression:

— . — . — . — . — . — . — . —

[He] mourned as he moved about the world,
deserted and alone, lamenting his unhappiness
day and night, until death's flood
brimmed up in his heart.

— . — . — . — . — . — . — . —

This is the cynicism that threatens America. The poem tells us that the dragon makes its home in the veteran's burial mound, but one doesn't have to think of the last veteran as dying. Rather, the funeral mound is his heart. America's heart has been taken over by a greedy, cynical, relentless dragon.

THE PERILS OF FIGHTING THE DRAGON

In addition to showing us how a country becomes possessed by the dragon, the poem also shows how dragon cynicism can infect those battling the dragon. Being a dragon fighter is hard, and just as the monster poisons Beowulf with a deadly bite, so it can poison those fighting for a more hopeful future. Put another way, even a dedicated hero is prone to despair. In its portrayal of the last days of Beowulf, the poem provides for us a description of the burned-out heroic reformer who becomes cynical.

Beowulf appears to be exhausted and despairing when the dragon attacks. Although for fifty years he has worked tirelessly for the Geats as their king, suddenly he is thrown into doubt:

> It [the dragon] threw the hero
> into deep anguish and darkened his mood:
> the wise man thought he must have thwarted
> ancient ordinance of the eternal Lord,
> broken His commandment. His mind was in turmoil,
> unaccustomed anxiety and gloom
> confused his brain . . .

It is frightening when idealists cease to believe in their country's future, especially when we have grown accustomed to looking to those idealists to shore up our own faith. We are dragged down when they start believing that all their past efforts have ultimately amounted to nothing. In Beowulf's case, he looks over his past and sees, not great victories against the monsters of resentment and grief, but only a string of meaningless deaths leading nowhere.

He remembers King Hrethel, his grandfather, who gave up and crawled into bed after his eldest son died in an accident. He remembers Hygelac, Hrethel's third son and Beowulf's uncle, who was killed by the Frisians. He remembers Hygelac's son Heardred, who was killed by the Swedes. Likewise, when Beowulf's nephew Wiglaf looks towards the future, he sees looming attacks from the Franks and the Frisians and final defeat at the hands of the Swedes. Victories are forgotten as though they never existed because they have led only to this moment of defeat and despair.

So should we conclude that America's century is over? Have our dragon billionaires and their minions irredeemably weakened us so that we must hand the keys of the future over to China? It's an ominous sign in the epic poem we have been studying that Beowulf ultimately is killed by the dragon.

Before he goes down, however, he teams up with a warrior from the next generation, grasps the sword of hope, and slays the monster. Yes, Beowulf dies, but he dies fighting for the future, and he leaves a young survivor who can carry on the fight. Beowulf may not live to see what comes next but he chooses to be a hero rather than a dragon and fights to liberate his people rather than to enrich himself. The poem gives us two armor-clad figures, a king and a monster, contending for the soul of the country, and it is the king, not the monster, who emerges victorious. Cynicism, in other words, is defeated. How we can draw on Beowulf's example and restore America's soul is set forth in the next chapter.

Chapter 6

BEOWULF'S RESPONSE: COLLECTIVE ACTION

Before I describe how Beowulf moves beyond cynicism and saves his country, let's remind ourselves of what is possible. An old warrior king and his young nephew—the poem calls them "partners in nobility"—come together to slay an implacable foe and liberate the hoarded treasure. What the young nephew Wiglaf then sees fills him with wonder:

—·—·—·—·—·—·—·—·—

a treasure-trove of astonishing richness,
wall-hangings that were a wonder to behold,
glittering gold spread across the ground . . .
          And he saw too a standard, entirely of gold,
hanging high over the hoard,
a masterpiece of filigree; it glowed with light
so he could make out the ground at his feet
and inspect the valuables.

—·—·—·—·—·—·—·—·—

Think of this treasure as not merely material goods but America's vast human potential, which will be released once wealth begins circulating again. Wiglaf is awed by the thrill and relief of overcoming dragon-induced sclerosis and discovering that his nation does indeed have a future. While previously he had seen Beowulf obsessing about the past, now he knows that warriors working together can liberate a rich treasure-trove of riches and revitalize a dispirited people. This is what it feels like to reconnect with hope.

What will it take for us to begin hoping again? Beowulf's last fight is the toughest of the three, for him and for us. Our fighting against Grendel and Grendel's Mother required us to win the hearts and minds of our fellow Americans, calling upon our national ideals and what is best in each of us. But defeating the dragon requires still more. It means advocating for economic policy changes that are guaranteed to arouse the dragon fury of entrenched interests, who will lash out with all their considerable firepower. Of the three battles, this is the most overtly political, which is why I focus in this chapter on legislative and electoral politics, especially at the presidential level.

The epic poem of a ninth-century feudal people cannot provide us with political details for our own late-capitalist democracy. And yet, *Beowulf* is still remarkably useful to use in our battle against our own dragons because the poem shows us how to conduct the battle—and how not to. The poem makes clear what kinds of tactics can defeat a greedy, cynical dragon, and, knowing that we will be hard-pressed in the fight, the poem also shows us how we can resist the downward pull of dragon cynicism within ourselves.

BEOWULF VS. DRAGON CYNICISM

Fighting dragons is exceedingly difficult, and Beowulf makes a series of mistakes before figuring out the right course of action. In our own political battles, we can learn as much from what Beowulf does wrong as from what he does right:

⟫→ he at first fails to acknowledge that his country has a dragon problem;

⟫→ once he finally admits the problem, he shows singular bravery in his willingness to take it on, but this bravery is itself problematic: rather than assembling all his troops to fight the

dragon, Beowulf mistakenly believes that he can solve the problem by himself;

⟫→ fighting the dragon single-handedly, Beowulf is over-
matched and eventually becomes infected with dragon poison;

⟫→ Beowulf's nephew, Wiglaf, representative of the next generation, takes the initiative, defying Beowulf's orders to leave the
battle to him. Rather than fleeing with the other Geat warriors,
Wiglaf joins in battle *with* Beowulf—a crucial step that turns the
tide against the dragon;

⟫→ the two warriors are finally able to kill the dragon because
they work together, with Beowulf protecting Wiglaf with his shield
and Wiglaf distracting the dragon with his sword. Wiglaf stabs
the monster in the belly and Beowulf finishes it off;

⟫→ a dying Beowulf sends Wiglaf off to survey the treasure cave
and bestows upon him a golden chain, suggesting that the young
must succeed the old and that their first duty in doing so is to
redistribute the wealth that the dragon—the old, greedy ruling
class—has kept from the rest of the nation.

It's not easy to admit that we have a dragon problem—which
is to say, that wealth has become so concentrated in the upper ech-
elons of society that it is stifling opportunities for everyone else.
Americans generally don't object that some people have much
more money than others. We reassure ourselves that there's
enough left over for the rest of us. After all, aren't we surrounded
by plenty of people living comfortable lives? Won't hard work and
initiative put us in their company?

Granted, this past recession has thrown many of us out of
work or into low-paying jobs, ravaged our retirement accounts,
and blocked the employment opportunities for young people. But
haven't we emerged from recessions before? Surely this one is an
aberration that won't happen again if we put certain measures in
place (although we then see lawmakers attempting to sabotage
even the relatively mild regulatory legislation that has been
passed). Surely a recovery is on its way that will stimulate business, replenish tax revenues, lead to rehiring teachers and public

sector workers, bring down the cost of higher education, restore slashed pensions, and refill depleted 401Ks. Although isn't this the second time in the past twelve years that a bursting bubble ravaged our retirement accounts?

In other words, the frequency and severity of economic downturns appear to be increasing, even as we remain unwilling to see how serious the problem has become. Our situation may have more in common with America before the Great Depression when income distribution was so askew that only significant wealth redistribution could (as people said at the time) "save capitalism." If America thinks that it can just coast into another "Morning in America" rather than engage in major restructuring, then we may be as delusional as Beowulf, who initially doesn't acknowledge that he is facing a new set of challenges:

——·——·——·——·——·——

He had scant regard
for the dragon as threat, no dread at all
of its courage or strength, for he had kept going
often in the past, though periods and ordeals
of every sort.

——·——·——·——·——·——

ACKNOWLEDGING THAT WE HAVE A DRAGON PROBLEM

It takes an outburst of dragon anger to alert Beowulf that his coasting days are over, just as over-the-top voter rage should alert contemporary America that the game has fundamentally changed. Following the strategy that the best defense is offense, the country's moneyed elite and their allies have doubled down on the policies that brought us the 2007 recession. The air is filled with dragon flames as certain politicians seek to shift wealth even further to the top 1 percent, whether by dismantling banking regulations, extending and increasing George W. Bush's high-end tax cuts, converting Medicare into a voucher program, or privatizing Social Security (although politicians stopped publicly advocating this idea after the 2007 recession).

One reason that so many of us want to avoid acknowledging the dragon is that its fire is fierce. Imagine the response if taxes were pushed up to 50% on the top earners (currently they are at 33%) or if the loopholes that allow certain companies and wealthy individuals to pay little or no taxes were abolished. Lesser heroes might be tempted to leave the dragon alone, allowing millionaires and billionaires to do what they do while the rest of us muddle along in a diminished America. This might be a particularly tempting course of action to pursue if we've cynically concluded that all government reform and all protests are bound to fail.

Our cynicism grows when our leaders seem to fail us, and Obama's performance against the dragon, like Beowulf's, has been mixed. When he first came into office, the president did not follow up his bold campaign rhetoric. Perhaps he feared the flames or didn't acknowledge their severity. Perhaps he underestimated dragon anger and thought that the monster could be placated. Or perhaps, as some of his leftist detractors accused, he was actually a dragon ally. In any event, President Obama did not nationalize the banks, pursue those financiers who had acted fraudulently, or push through a stimulus package large enough to turn back the tide of recession (although the stimulus package that *was* enacted was still the largest in history). Having lost the offensive, Obama saw banks refuse to lend, Wall Street fight fiercely against even modest regulation, and the country's recovery falter.

Beowulf's initial mishandling of the dragon also cues us into another possible Obama mistake: he may have overestimated his personal power. The outlines of this common leadership failing are shown to us through Beowulf's speech to his men when he tells them that he will fight the dragon alone:

—·—·—·—·—·—·—·—

Men-at-arms, remain here on the barrow,
safe in your armor, to see which one of us
is better in the end at bearing wounds
in a deadly fray. The fight is not yours,
nor is it up to any man except me
to measure his strength against the monster
or to prove his worth. I shall win the gold
by my courage, or else mortal combat,
doom of battle, will bear your lord away.

—·—·—·—·—·—·—·—

Beowulf may seem to be a caring leader here, promising his men
that they will be safe if he leaves them behind, but instead he dis-
empowers them by his go-it-alone attitude so that they scatter when
the battle goes against him. In Obama's case, he may have thought
that the mediation methods he developed as community organizer
and senator could work when he was president. At times early in his
presidency, he appeared to think he could hover above the fray of
party politics rather than relying on his Democratic comrades as
the battle raged. He didn't involve his followers as much as was
once envisioned (say, through social media). Nor did he use his considerable rhetorical skills to rally the nation to his side. At times he
appears to have thought that if he could quietly and diligently get
things done, the country would reward him for his efforts.

The dragon responded, in dragon fashion, with increased rage
and greed, and we have witnessed a non-stop rightwing temper
tantrum ever since. Any illusions that the president could placate
or circumvent dragon wrath were definitively put to rest in the
summer of 2011. At that point, Obama found himself enmeshed
in the dragon's coils as he tried to persuade angry House members
not to send the county into credit default. As his approval ratings
dropped to the 40 percent range, he learned, perhaps definitively
this time, that his individual sword thrusts were insufficient and
that dragons are not interested in compromise.

THE NEED
FOR COALITIONS

The mark of great leaders is not so much that they avoid mistakes but that they learn from them. Obama can take a lesson from Beowulf, who realizes that he must allow Wiglaf to help him and who gives him the protection of his shield. The poem also provides guidance to Obama's potential allies, without whom the president cannot succeed.

The poem shows us two kinds of allies. We can think of the first, those who allow their king to fight the dragon alone, as the voters who thought they could elect Obama president and then let him do the rest of the work. Beowulf's warriors have even more reason to trust in their king than do Obama's followers: Obama was a newly elected politician president trying to govern amidst an explicit rightwing attempt to derail his presidency whereas Beowulf has successfully ruled his people for 50 years, all the while keeping foreign invaders at bay.

Both Beowulf and Obama were quickly deserted, however, at the first blast of dragon fire. In both cases, those who might have been expected to support their leader instead threw up their hands and became demoralized.

These allies could be those progressives who campaigned for Obama but became disillusioned with him for not being bolder or more liberal and who now are prepared to drop out of the political process. Or maybe they are the moderates, including moderate Republicans, who voted for the president, blamed him for the subsequent dragon fury, urged him to compromise with the dragon and, when that didn't work, concluded that he wasn't up to the job.

Wiglaf is the prototype of the other kind of ally, the one who wades into the flames when they are at their hottest. A key turning point in Obama's fortunes came with the rise of the Occupy Wall Street movement, which gave the president the footing he needed to reinvoke his campaign's vision of hope for all Americans and to go on the offensive. Although many of the protesters were severely critical of the president, he listened to what they had to say and was able to use their activism as his own motivation to change the conversation and become more critical of "the 1 percent."

The parallels between the Beowulf-Wiglaf collaboration and the Obama-OWS dynamics help us see what we as foot soldiers must do. Before people took to the streets, the momentum appeared to be with rightwing Republicans and their threatened dragonlike budget reductions. The president, reeling from dragon fire, appeared willing to accede to large cuts to Medicare and other social programs, causing his supporters to scatter. After the OWS demonstrations, however, the focus of the entire nation's political discourse shifted to economic inequality, which could well be the major issue of campaign 2012.

WARRIORS STEPPING UP

We can learn from Wiglaf, a young warrior witnessing his first fighting, that the important thing is not our own disillusionment but the battle itself. Regardless of how our leaders have disappointed us, Wiglaf teaches us that it is still our responsibility to engage with them against a common enemy. Its destructive power, after all, is far more significant than any mistakes our leaders might have made.

Like many Obama supporters, Wiglaf knows that his leader has brought some of his problems on himself. He even points out that his king insisted on going his own way, with serious consequences:

Often when one man follows his own will
many are hurt.

Nevertheless, Wiglaf goes to Beowulf's rescue anyway, seeing it as his job to bolster the man who leads his people. Wiglaf's speech shows the potential for youthful idealism to reinvigorate the elderly:

—.—.—.—.—.—.—.—

Go on, dear Beowulf, do everything
you said you would when you were still young
and vowed you would never let your name and fame
be dimmed while you lived. Your deeds are famous,
so stay resolute, my lord, defend your life now
with the whole of your strength. I shall stand by you.

—.—.—.—.—.—.—.—

The message of Beowulf-Wiglaf's victory is that neither leader nor allies can defeat the dragon alone. A criticism of OWS has been that it lacks an effective entry into politics—fearful of tainting their hands with politics, some look only to demonstrations and are reluctant to collaborate with less-than-perfect heroes. Many demonstrators have been anarchists who, in the American individualist tradition, are suspicious of all political institutions. They and other progressives can learn from Wiglaf that, to achieve their ends, they need Beowulf's shield (in their case the power of the presidency), just as the president needs their powerful swords chopping away at the monster. If the OWS protestors don't learn this, they are in as much danger of cynicism as the disillusioned voters who fled from Obama two years earlier.

Beowulf's fight reminds us that there will be moments of discouragement: he is bitten by the dragon as the fight progresses and temporarily loses heart. In the end, however, the poem gives us the inspiring sight of two warriors joining forces and slaying the beast:

—.—.—.—.—.—.—.—

They had killed the enemy, courage quelled his life;
that pair of kinsmen, partners in nobility,
had destroyed the foe. So every man should act,
be at hand when needed . . .

—.—.—.—.—.—.—.—

Wiglaf's criticism indicates that it's okay to be critical of one's leader. In fact, one has a responsibility to be so. But one should be critical in a way that supports the cause of progress. Franklin Roosevelt once told a group of disillusioned leftists to continue putting pressure on him because otherwise he would not be able to continue to pursue a progressive agenda. Although liberals today revere Roosevelt for the New Deal, he would not have enacted many of his signature programs had he not been pushed to do so by a left-leaning Congress. His "we have nothing to fear but fear itself" speech came *after* he'd been president for four years, and even then he wasn't impervious to dragon influence.

To cite a revealing instance, according to Keynesian economist Paul Krugman the headway Roosevelt made against the Great Depression experienced a significant setback in 1937 when, panicked by a growing deficit, he engaged in "premature austerity," plunging the country back into depression. Whenever times are bad, our leaders are tempted to succumb to their dragon tendencies. They need the clarity and insistence of the American populace to resist becoming cynical.

If Obama doesn't seem a perfect hero, the poem gives us a lesson on that as well. When we fixate on a hero from the past like FDR rather than acknowledging that politics is a human process involving flawed humans, we give rise to another kind of dragon. After Beowulf dies, the treasure that he liberated is buried with him and a shrine, doubling as a lighthouse, is raised above it. The poem laments what happens to the gold:

— ·— ·— ·— ·— ·— ·—

> They let the ground keep that ancestral treasure,
> gold under gravel, gone to earth,
> as useless to men now as it ever was.

— ·— ·— ·— ·— ·— ·—

The shrine built for Beowulf may seem to provide a lighthouse that will guide future sailors over "dark seas." Our past heroes can indeed function as models and sources of inspiration. But if we turn them into fetishes, we cease to look to ourselves for answers and leave ourselves vulnerable. *Beowulf* ends in lamentation over the end of Geatland as a nation. With their king gone, Wiglaf sees his people as the ready prey of the Swedes, Franks, and Frisians.

Nor is it only our leaders that we risk fetishizing. If we turn a particular image of America into an idol—if, say, we listen to empty slogans about how America can dominate the world as it did in the aftermath of World War II—then we, like Beowulf, are looking backward, not forward. Just because the America of the 21st century will look much different than the America of the 20th doesn't mean that it can't be a vibrant nation.

It seems appropriate to end this chapter by turning our attention to the next generation. Looking around him, Wiglaf sees disheartened followers who have relied on Beowulf to provide them with comfortable lives and who then, when things go sour, flee the scene. What he says to them he could say to all of us as we prepare to go forth against the dragon fire that the 2012 general election will offer up:

—·—·—·—·—·—·—

> [N]ow the day has come
> when this lord we serve needs sound men
> to give him their support. Let us go to him,
> help our leader through the hot flame
> and dread of the fire. As God is my witness,
> I would rather my body were robed in the same
> burning blaze as my gold-giver's body
> than go back home bearing arms.

—·—·—·—·—·—·—

The flames will indeed be hot, especially as Super Pacs with unprecedented amounts of money unleash their attacks. Americans will be tempted to yield to cynicism, throw up their hands, and run for cover. Wiglaf reminds us what heroes can accomplish when they stand up for their country in the face of dragon attacks. Working together, we can free up "a treasure-trove of astonishing richness."

EPILOGUE

People can become monster-like when their economic expectations come under attack. The widening income gap and hollowing out of the middle class are prompting Americans to rage against others who are superficially different from them, closing their eyes to the humanity of their fellow citizens. In the process, they deny their own humanity, which is the very definition of monstrosity.

There are many unscrupulous conmen and women out there who will stoke our fears for their own selfish ends, less concerned with the health of the republic than with getting us to watch their shows, buy their books, swell their membership, and vote for them. They are less concerned with the good of the nation than with protecting the economic and political power of the 1 percent. In these difficult economic times, people are particularly vulnerable to demagogic appeals and prejudicial scapegoating. Thanks to the *Citizens United* Supreme Court decision, the hucksters have unprecedented amounts of money to increase the hysteria.

Fear and anger are compelling emotions that, by their volume and force, threaten to overwhelm rational, measured responses. As I noted in the Grendel chapters, those possessed by anger can seem ten feet tall and unstoppable. If we are to fight to make sure that America lives up to the American Dream, then we must become citizen warriors and resist backing down before our fellow citizens when they exhibit troll behavior. We are called upon to marshal the self-discipline to respond effectively, which means not reacting with angry sword thrusts of our own. We must deal with our grief in healthy ways as we work with those of our fellow citizens who are thrashing around in their own unexamined grief. Above all, we must resist the lure of cynicism, the temptation to walk away from the battle insisting that it can never be won.

Always we must remember that, while the battle sometimes seems daunting, it is less so when we work in concert with others. There are few activities more exhilarating than joining with a group of fellow citizens to build a better society. The dragon's hoard has wealth sufficient for all of us if we marshal up the collective will to liberate it.

As I write these words in April of 2012, Republicans and Democrats each face specific challenges that demand heroic responses. Those Republicans who have not surrendered to rightwing extremism need to keep pushing for moderation in whatever ways they can. They must call out Grendelian resentment whenever they encounter it, chastising fellow Republicans who scapegoat illegal immigrants, American Muslims, gay and lesbian Americans, and African Americans, among others. Moderate Republicans must resist the urge to become hysterical about their own grieving. They must, above all, do what they can to convince their party not to make drastic cuts to the social safety nets ("hammocks" as some in their party deride them) and not to move ever more of the country's riches upward to the very wealthy. Perhaps these moderate Republicans might point out that Henry Ford made millions by insuring that his workers had enough money to buy the cars they made.

Granted, moderates will find themselves under dragon fire if they call for a more equitable distribution of the country's riches. Heroes don't always reap immediate rewards. But if they stay strong, sooner or later they will attract Wiglafs to their side.

Democrats and Progressives, meanwhile, need to extend a hand to all Americans, even as their grip remains firm with principled conviction. They must remind themselves that they have access to a giant sword—America's belief in fair play—which will come to their aid when things look bad. They must find allies as they fight to lessen the income gaps.

Amongst those allies are America's youth, our Wiglafs. Occupy Wall Street captured young people's imaginations because their ideal America is not a country where the 1 percent commands most of the country's wealth. This idealism can potentially reinvigorate those political leaders who are willing to listen to this call for economic and political justice in America. In part because of the Occupy Wall Street demonstrations, Obama shifted his agenda from debt reduction to income equity. It's up to Wiglaf to support a president who has made this shift and to spur him on to ever more effective measures against our dragons.

The general election of 2012 involves a very clear choice. A man who has captured the imagination of the historically disenfranchised will be facing a CEO of a private equity firm that practices a harsh form of capitalism. Obama has presented himself as champion of the middle class as well as the poor while Romney has embraced a Ryan budget that promises severe cuts to programs for the vulnerable and sizeable tax breaks for the wealthy. Warrior work at this juncture involves knocking on doors, making phone calls, writing letters, giving money, and voting. Obama may have strayed at times into dragon realms, but Wiglaf's criticism of Beowulf demonstrates that one can be critical and supportive of the president at the same time.

So America, can we heed the call of the hero? When Grendelian resentment comes storming at us, can we hold fast to those values of inclusiveness that are enshrined in our Constitution, emblazoned on the Statue of Liberty, and lauded in such literary masterpieces as *Leaves of Grass, Huckleberry Finn, The Grapes of Wrath,* and *Beloved*? When Grendel's Mother, heart-wounded, sinks her claws into us and pulls us into deep despair, can we remember that we have ideals that are bigger than we are? And when dragon gloom threatens to burn us with its wrath and inject us with its poison, can we remember that we have each other?

The bad news is that monsters teem all around us and have become ever fiercer as income gaps have widened and the 1 percent has grown stronger. The good news is that each one of us has Beowulf and Wiglaf potential. I believe that we can defeat our monsters, just as the Geat warriors defeated theirs, if we keep a firm grip, wield the sword of fairness, resist the flames of dragon despair, and stand strong together. The battle before us is a battle worthy of a great people.

BEOWULF:
AN OVERVIEW

The poem was composed (some think orally, some written) somewhere between the 8th and the 11th centuries in Anglo-Saxon England. It is set centuries earlier in Scandinavia. Beowulf is a young warrior from Geatland (now southern Sweden) who journeys to the kingdom of the Danes, the regional super power, to battle the giant troll Grendel. Grendel hates it when others are happy and has been attacking the mead hall of the powerful Danish king Hrothgar. Beowulf is greeted as a hero but is challenged by Unferth, one of King Hrothgar's warriors who is jealous of the attention the young man is receiving. Beowulf's assertive response silences Unferth, and he then backs up his words by defeating Grendel, grabbing his arm so tightly that the troll panics and rips himself free of his limb, sustaining a mortal wound.

The following morning the warriors track Grendel to the lake to which he has fled. On their way back, the bard tells the story of Beowulf's feat and then sings of two legendary kings, the good king Sigemund and the bad king Heremod. Later at a celebratory feast, the bard tells another story, this one about a diplomatic marriage between the Frisian king Finn and the Danish princess Hildebuhr that failed to hold the peace. According to the story, renewed fighting broke out between the Frisians and the Danes and, given the lack of a clear resolution, the two sides had to live together for a winter until the Danes rose up in vengeance and killed King Finn.

Also at the meal, Danish Queen Wealtheow, while proving a gracious hostess, is worried that King Hrothgar will name Beowulf as his successor in place of their two young sons. To forestall this from happening, she flatters Beowulf and also expresses her confidence in the king's nephew Hrothulf, who would become prince regent should Hrothgar die early. We learn from hints in the poem that she has reason to be worried and that Regent Hrothulf will seize the throne after Hrothgar dies.

That night the mead hall experiences a retaliatory attack, this from Grendel's mother. She kills the king's best friend, Aeschere, before fleeing back to her lake. Beowulf tracks her there, dives in, and battles with her in her underwater hall. The struggle is fierce but he finally manages to kill her with a giant sword that he finds.

In a second celebratory feast, we hear more talk about the bad king Heremod, and King Hrothgar also delivers a cautionary account about how successful kings can become overly proud and isolated from their people.

Beowulf at this point returns home, where he shares his winnings with his sovereign and uncle, the Geat king Hygelac. Hygelac rewards Beowulf generously in return. When Hygelac dies, Queen Hygd offers the throne to Beowulf over her son Heardred, but Beowulf defers, serving instead as regent until Heardred grows up. Only when Heardred is killed in battle does Beowulf, who is next in line, assume the kingship.

Beowulf reigns successfully for fifty years, but the end of his reign is blighted by a dragon that lives in the funeral mound of "the last veteran," the last surviving member of a great race of warriors. The dragon is roused into anger by the theft of a cup, and he eventually burns down Beowulf's hall. In his anguish over the dragon attacks, Beowulf thinks back to how the preceding Geat kings have died: his grandfather Hrethel died of grief when his eldest son was accidentally killed by his second son, his uncle Hygelac was killed by the Frisians, and his cousin Heardred was killed by the Swedes.

Ordering his men to stand back so as to leave all the glory to him, Beowulf takes on the dragon alone but is overwhelmed and manages to kill it only with the help of his nephew Wiglaf, who comes to his aid when the others flee. Beowulf sustains a poisonous dragon bite and dies after liberating the treasure, which is buried beneath a coastal shrine that will double as a lighthouse for sailors. Seeing into the future, Wiglaf notes that, with Beowulf dead, the Geats are now vulnerable to hostile neighbors and foresees that his people will be overrun by the Swedes.

LIST OF PRINCIPLE CHARACTERS

Beowulf – Young Geat warrior and eventual king of Geatland.

Finn (bard's tale) - King of the Frisians who, in a diplomatic marriage that eventually fails in its purpose, marries Hildebuhr of the Danes. After renewed fighting breaks out and both Finn's Danish brother-in-law and his son are killed, Finn tries to maintain a delicate peace but is eventually killed when Hengest, a second brother-in-law, rises up.

Dragon – Moves into the treasure hoard of "the last veteran" and attacks the surrounding countryside after a cup is stolen, burning down Beowulf's hall.

Grendel and Grendel's Mother - Giant trolls that live in an underwater hall and that attack Heorot, King Hrothgar's mead hall.

Heardred – Beowulf's cousin and king. Beowulf serves as regent to the young Heardred and becomes king when Heardred is killed by the Swedes.

Heremod (bard's tale) – Legendary greedy king.

Hildebuhr (bard's tale) – Danish wife of the Frisian king Finn, who sees her Danish brother and her Frisian son killed when the diplomatic marriage fails to hold so that renewed fighting breaks out between the two kingdoms.

Hrethel (Beowulf recollection)– Geat king and Beowulf's grandfather, who dies of grief after his second son accidentally kills his eldest.

Hrothgar – King of Denmark who builds the magnificent Heorot Hall, target of Grendel's attacks.

Hrothulf - Hrothgar's nephew who, as prince regent after Hrothgar's death (and after Beowulf is gone), seizes the throne.

Hygelac – King of the Geats, Beowulf's sovereign, who is eventually killed by the Frisians.

Last Veteran – Last survivor of a "highborn race" whose treasure-filled burial mound becomes the dragon's home.

Sigemund (bard's tale) – Legendary good king.

Unferth - Blustering Danish warrior who sits at Hrothgar's feet.

Wealtheow – Hrothgar's queen who dissuades her husband from naming Beowulf his heir.

Wiglaf - Young Geat warrior and Beowulf's nephew who helps him kill the dragon.

WORKS CITED

Brooks, David. "The Possum Republicans." *New York Times.* New York Times, 27 Feb. 2012. Web.

Chait, Jonathan. "The Roots of the Court's Obamacare Panic." *NYMag.com.* New York Magazine, 29 March 2012. Web.

Dowd, Maureen. "Pass the Caribou Stew." *New York Times.* New York Times, 7 Dec. 2010. Web.

Fouche, Gwladys. "Special Report: Life after Breivik." Reuters, 15 April 2012. Web.

Frank, Thomas. *Crashing the Tea Party: Mass Media and the Campaign to Remake American Politics.* Boulder; London: Paradigm, 2011. Print.

Greenstein, Robert. "Statement of Robert Greenstein, President, on Chairman Ryan's Budget Plan." Center on Budget and Policy Priorities, 21 March 2012. Web.

Heaney, Seamus. Beowulf: *A New Verse Translation.* New York: W. W. Norton, 2001.

Jones, Van. *Rebuild the Dream.* New York: Nation Books, 2012. Print.

King, Colbert I. "The Demonizing of Barack Obama." *Washington Post.* Washington Post, 4 Feb. 2012. Web.

Krugman, Paul. "Keynes Was Right." *New York Times.* New York Times, 9 Dec. 2011. Web.

Lizza, Ryan. "The Obama Memos: The Making of a Post-Post-Partisan Presidency. *New Yorker,* 30 Jan. 2012: 36-49. Print.

Mann, Thomas E. and Norman J Ornstein. *It's Even Worse Than It Looks: How the American Constitutional System Collided with the New Politics of Extremism*. New York: Basic Books, 2012. Print.

Plutarch. *Lives*. 1928. Trans. Bernadotte Perrin. Vol. 1. Cambridge: Harvard UP; London: William Heinemann, 1982. Print. 11 vols.

Reich, Robert B. *Aftershock: The Next Economy and America's Future*. New York: Alfred A. Knopf, 2010. Print.

—. "The Widening Wealth Divide, and Why We Need a Surtax on the Super Wealthy." March 13, 2012. *HuffingtonPost.com*. Huffington Post, 13 March 2010. Web.

Saez, Emmanuel. "Striking It Richer: The Evolution of Top Incomes in the United States (Updated with 2009 and 2010 estimates)." PDF file.

Sullivan, Andrew. "How Obama's Long Game Will Outsmart His Critics." *Newsweek*. The Daily Beast, 16 Jan. 2012. Web.

—. "Seeing Obama through the Civil Rights Prism." *Thedailybeast.com*. The Daily Beast, 14 Aug. 2011. Web.

Street, Paul and Anthony DiMaggio. *Crashing the Tea Party: Mass Media and the Campaign to Remake American Politics*. Boulder; London: Paradigm Publishers, 2011. Print.

Sutton, Robert. *The No Asshole Rule: Building a Civilized Workplace and Surviving One That Isn't*. New York: Warner Business Books, 2007. Print.

ABOUT THE AUTHOR

Robin Bates is Professor of English at St. Mary's College of Maryland in St. Mary's City, where he has been teaching English language literature, including *Beowulf*, for over 30 years. Robin was also a journalist for two years, and before coming to St. Mary's he taught for a year at Morehouse College in Atlanta. Raised in Sewanee, Tennessee, he received his B.A. from Carleton College and his M.A. and PhD from Emory University, where he studied under J. Paul Hunter. He has published numerous articles, many on film, dealing with questions of audience response, and he has twice received Fulbright fellowships to Slovenia. His posts on literature and life appear daily on his blog *Better Living through Beowulf: How Classic Literature Can Change Your Life* at betterlivingthroughbeowulf.com. Robin is married to Julia, an educator, and they have three sons, Justin (deceased), Darien and Tobias.